Handle with Care

*Managing Difficult
Situations in Schools with
Dignity and Respect*

Jimmy Casas
Joy Kelly

ConnectEDD Publishing
Chicago, Illinois

Praise for *Handle with Care*

Best-selling author Jimmy Casas and Joy Kelly share powerful and relevant stories in *Handle with Care: Managing Difficult Situations in Schools with Dignity and Respect.* They remind us that the heart and soul of a healthy culture begins and ends with the way we handle all members of a school community with care, grace, and dignity. This book is filled with heartfelt, practical advice and will serve as a reflection guide for educators for years to come.

    —Jon Gordon, Best-Selling Author of *The Energy Bus* and *The Power of Positive Leadership*

Handle with Care is the perfect read for any educator in need of some inspiration and guidance, especially in this current era as we navigate unprecedented challenges. As a special education instructional assistant, I can honestly say every educator can benefit from this book—regardless of title or wheelhouse. Casas and Kelly provide well balanced doses of relatable anecdotes that have changed my perspective on some of my own past experiences and have prepared me for those that have yet to come. After reading this book, I am left with the confidence that no student is too hard to reach, and no barrier is too high to overcome.

    —Jamileh Abu-Ghannum, Special Education Instructional Assistant

Inspiring and empowering! I feel like I was just gifted decades of experience from culture of excellence leaders. This is an essential, compelling, and actionable guide for creating a positive school culture where learners of all ages thrive. Casas and Kelly masterfully navigate complex issues with empathy, servant spirit, and respect. Vignettes shared throughout reveal blind spots and the keys to conversations that repair damaged relationships and nurture healthy ones. If you are ready for next-level leadership characterized by courage, integrity, and grace, this book is required reading.

—**Lainie Rowell**, lead author of *Evolving Learner* and international education consultant

If we want all students to reach beyond their own expectations, then we need to make sure that our interactions with them are more human, especially those students who do not always make it easy. In *Handle with Care*, Casas and Kelly offer important insight into turning those difficult situations into impactful learning experiences.

—**Peter DeWitt**, Ed.D. School Leadership Coach/Facilitator of Learning *Finding Common Ground* Blog (*Education Week*)

Powerful, Real, Timely! *Handle with Care* is loaded with practical applications, opportunities for genuine reflection, and awesome culture builders you can implement right now. At a time when it may be more important than ever, Casas and Kelly lay down a challenge for all leaders to push past surface-level assumptions and think deeply about school culture. Through the impact of word choice, a focus on authentic relationships, or a call to empower every adult and student, *Handle with Care* will inspire leaders to walk in purpose for their entire school community.

—**Darrin M Peppard**, Ed.D., Educator, Author, Speaker, Leadership Consultant

Authors Jimmy Casas and Joy Kelly do not shy away from our most challenging situations in their new book *Handle with Care: Managing Difficult Situations in Schools with Dignity and Respect*. The "Eyes on Culture in Action" sections offer sound strategies for building better school cultures in almost every area. The scenarios and strategies found in the book are firmly grounded in the reality of today's educators and students. If you have been looking for an educational book that demonstrates a full understanding of the challenges facing educators today while also providing strategies for dealing with these challenges, then look no further than *Handle with Care*. If you can only make time to read one educational book during this hectic year, it must be *Handle with Care*, but don't just read it. Re-read it. Implement strategies from it. Live it, and use it to make your classroom, school, or district a joyous place filled with care, dignity, and respect for all.

> —**Stoney M. Beavers**, Ph.D., Assistant Director of the Alabama Best Practices Center, Former Assistant Superintendent for Blount County Schools

Jimmy + Joy + a Culturizing Mindset + Supportive & Demanding Leaders + Empathy + Grit + Grace + Gratitude = a catalytic read & resource for schools & districts to...THRIVE! #Read #Heed. #Cutlurize #KeepGoing

> —**Kevin Carroll**, author/speaker/instigator of inspiration

Handle with Care speaks to a necessary element of excellence in schools. Excellence is not just about high academic standards. In fact, high standards won't work if the tone and spirit of the school culture isn't both caring and supportive. Schools face so many tragic situations and are expected to navigate often very troubling scenarios. *Handle with Care* offers readers insight into the right attitudes and dispositions to bring to difficult conditions and provides practical strategies for building a culture of grace and greatness. It's a must read for all educators at every level.

> —**T. J. Vari**, Assistant Superintendent, Appoquinimink School District

Handle with Care is an excellent book which focuses on how educators can manage difficult situations with the dignity and respect that every single student deserves. Oftentimes at school and in life, we only see what is above the surface of the water. There is so much happening below the surface and that is certainly the case with many of our students. This must-read book explores the strategies, stories, and experiences which will allow every educator to dive beneath the surface of the water to connect with their students in a way to handle them with dignity and respect, no matter what lies beneath.

—**Randy L. Russell**, Superintendent, Freeman, WA

Handle with Care describes the empathy that our schools need now more than ever before. Jimmy and Joy remind us that we are in the people business and the only way we will improve our schools, address inequities, and help students learn is if we are mindful of how we handle the most sensitive and emotional interactions with the educators we supervise, our students, and the rest of our school community. They provide an array of scenarios and their suggested action steps will help any leader demonstrate empathy and care. It is through these steps that we can create a stronger, more vibrant, and caring culture.

—**Henry J. Turner**, Principal, Newton North High School

As educators, we work in an environment where every interaction matters and the sum total of those interactions has the opportunity to impact the culture of a school. A challenging part of our job as educators is handling difficult situations in a meaningful and caring way that allows all involved to leave the situation as better versions of ourselves. In this book by Casas and Kelly, educators are offered practical advice, wisdom, and strategies for how to deal with demanding situations with empathy and compassion, fostering a culture of excellence.

—**Patrick R. Keenoy**, Ph.D., principal, Rogers Elementary School, St. Louis, MO

If school leaders are looking for an opportunity to reflect on their current leadership and culture practices, *Handle with Care* is the book to read. Using practical situations that we face every day, Jimmy and Joy encourage you to see multiple perspectives and the impact on culture. With each page, you will discover clear and actionable strategies to bring a more respectful and elevated tone to your entire campus. *Handle with Care* is a must read for every educator!

    —**Shana Henry**, Ed.D., principal and host of the *Principals of Success* podcast

As educators, we never know what students have endured or faced in their personal lives that truly impacts their educational experiences. *Handle with Care* addresses the complexities that both teachers and administrators face when it comes to understanding the individual needs of every student as they navigate mental health issues, including death, financial challenges, depression, and anxiety. In order for educators to be true agents of change, we must be comfortable with disrupting the status quo and fostering authentic equitable environments for all students to thrive. Each chapter unpacks a core principle, real educational vignettes, as well as practical and realistic takeaways and reflective questions that help educators take the next steps towards culturizing their practices. This is the perfect book and resource for every educator and their team that is serious about fostering inclusive learning environments for all students!

    —**Dr. Basil Marin**, HS Assistant Principal/DEI Consultant, Atlanta, GA

Handle with Care provides real solutions to real challenges that educators face daily. Through the authentic vignettes that are shared, along with the reflective questions and tone of the book, Jimmy and Joy are able to connect with readers. This connection makes *Handle with Care* read like a conversation instead of a book. This resource is a go-to for educators as they navigate challenges and remove barriers to ensure that students and staff feel emotionally safe and supported at school.

Handle with Care focuses on the most important aspect of the school experience—Relationships.

   —Sanée Bell, Ed.D, Author of *Be Excellent on Purpose: Intentional Strategies for Impactful Leadership*

A bookmarked copy of *Handle with Care* needs to be on the desk of every teacher and leader working in schools today! Each of the core principles discussed are faced numerous times throughout the year by educators and include specific steps to consider for keeping student needs and culture at the forefront of our thoughts and actions. The clear tips and strategies included for responding to potentially disruptive situations provide educators and leaders with avenues to prevent communication breakdowns and encourage respect, kindness, and understanding. *Handle with Care* demonstrates practical areas where we can be reflective of our situations and make changes to better serve everyone!

   —Kristen Bordonaro, Special Education Administrator

As a new administrator, *Handle with Care* is the perfect guide for navigating challenging situations with teachers and students. Jimmy and Joy remind us that it's easy to let our emotions take the lead, but with practice, we can put aside shame and act instead with grace and compassion.

   —Autumn Zaminski, Assistant Principal, Apple Distinguished Educator

This amazing book embraces the daily challenges of our jobs as administrators in both respectful and dignified ways so that we can maintain a positive school or district culture. Jimmy Casas and Joy Kelly write an engaging narrative that shares painfully honest and challenging school vignettes that speak to relevant topics in our schools in dealing with social justice, student voice, and difficult situations. The "Eyes on Culture in Action" sections assist educators with being self-reflective. This book leaves you energized with a charge to go forth on your journey and make a difference in a positive way today, tomorrow, and always.

—**Julia Wall**, Elementary Curriculum Coordinator, Director of
OSR Pre-K, Limestone County Schools

Casas and Kelly knock it out of the park with their latest book, *Handle with Care*. As educators, we often don't talk about the difficult situations that make our stomachs drop or our pulse quicken; however, Jimmy and Joy do so in a way that is approachable and relatable while providing easy-to-implement strategies to help get you through. This book should be required reading for all educators. We never know what will come our way and we must handle all students and staff with care.

—**Dr. Rachael George**, Co-author of *PrinicpalED*, speaker,
NAESP Fellow, and educational leader

Handle with Care comes at the perfect time for today's educators. The title captures our opportunity and challenge to educate and lead in this uncertain world. We all know social and emotional learning is a priority, yet we are all wondering about how to get started, who needs our help, and where it all fits in the school calendar. Well, Jimmy Casas and Joy Kelly deliver the solution our schools need in this wonderfully written and compassionate read. Your school's culture will be transformed.

—**Kelly Croy**, Director of Innovation and Instruction for Port
Clinton City Schools and Host of *The Wired Educator* Podcast

For educators who are champions for all students or want to be, *Handle with Care* is a must read!! Jimmy Casas and Joy Kelly target our assumptions and allow us to see the world from our students' perspectives. By giving real-world examples and strategies to help deal with behavior with dignity, this book helps educators re-discover the "why" behind their practices and refine them in a way to ensure that students are successful. I highly recommend this timely and necessary handbook as it should be in the hands of all in the education profession. Especially now, we need to understand our students, staff, and families and build relationships in order to keep our promises and lead and teach with empathy and grace.

—**Jenny Nauman**, Assistant Superintendent, Cape Henlopen School District, 2016 National Distinguished Principal

Handle with Care by Jimmy Casas and Joy Kelly is a masterclass of teachable moments and usable strategies for educational leaders and classroom teachers alike to implement within their schools while working through disruptive situations with students. It focuses on looking further than the moment to use disruptions as opportunities to teach and learn. This book provides educators a path to go beyond the call and teach beyond the walls of the classroom, providing strategies for building relationships that empower our students.

—**Jonathan Alsheimer**, Teacher, Speaker, Author of *Next Level Teaching*

This publication is available at discount pricing when purchased in quantity for educational purposes, promotions, or fundraisers. For inquiries and details, contact the publisher at
info@connecteddpublishing.com

Published by ConnectEDD Publishing LLC
Chicago, IL
www.connecteddpublishing.com

Cover Design: Kheila Dunkerly

Handle with Care: Managing Difficult Situations in Schools with Dignity and Respect/ Jimmy Casas and Joy Kelly. —1st ed.
Paperback ISBN 978-1-7361996-1-9
Ebook ISBN 978-1-7361996-2-6

Dedication

Jimmy: This book is dedicated to my former administrative teammates who supported me throughout my twenty-two years as a school leader. The countless challenges we encountered and worked through together shaped me into becoming the leader I always wanted to be. It is because of them that I continue to serve others in this noble profession that we call school leadership.

Joy: This book is dedicated to my mom, my first teacher and best model for how to handle difficult situations with care and love ❤

With profound gratitude, I also thank the many students and educators who serve as champions for inclusion, respect, and kindness. I have been blessed by your example.

Table of Contents

Foreword

In 2017, Jimmy Casas published *Culturize: Every Student. Every Day. Whatever It Takes.*, which quickly became one of the best-selling education books of the modern era. Since writing *Culturize*, Casas has spoken to thousands of educators around the country, elaborating on central themes of the book and providing strategies for enacting practices in schools and districts everywhere designed to achieve the types of schools we need for our children in the 21st century. The four core "Culturize" principles Casas writes and speaks about are simple, yet profound: As educators, we must (1) Champion for Students (2) Expect Excellence (3) Carry the Banner and (4) Be a Merchant of Hope. However, it is not enough that individual educators exhibit these behaviors; instead, we must create cultures in which all school community members are dedicated to these four core principles. Creating a culture of caring, kind, honest, and compassionate educators designed to challenge and inspire each member of the school community to become more than they ever thought possible is the overarching intent behind the *Culturize* philosophy.

In addition to the thousands of educators who have heard Casas speak and who have read his books, many schools and districts have also conducted book studies based on *Culturize*. As a result, in 2020, ConnectEDD Publishing created a *Culturize Action Guide* to serve as a resource for educators embarking on such book studies. The *Action Guide* is designed to serve as a road map for taking specific action steps as a school community based on the ideas found in *Culturize*. However, perhaps the most rewarding response from educators who have read and been inspired by the book has come from those who have shared their stories of taking the principles from *Culturize* and incorporating them into their classrooms, schools, and districts. Many teachers, principals, and district office leaders have shared stories so powerful that we decided to ask them to formalize these stories in book format and the idea for a limited series of books based on *Culturize* was born.

In thinking of a title for this series, we started with the premise that the focus of *Culturize* is, of course, "culture," and that we should constantly be "looking at" and examining our current culture juxtaposed with our desired culture and doing everything we can to close the gap from "status quo" to "desired status." And, just as we often need "all hands on deck" when it comes to the work we do, we also need "all eyes on culture" when it comes to ensuring excellence throughout our schools and districts; thus, the series, *Eyes On Culture*. The book you are about to read is the second in this series and we could not be more proud of it as well as the first book in the series, *Multiply Excellence in Your School* by Emily Paschall. In *Handle with Care*, by Jimmy Casas and Joy Kelly, the authors examine a variety of difficult situations that arise in schools everywhere during any school year. They share stories about these difficult-to-handle situations and offer specific, practical ideas for handling such delicate situations with dignity, respect...and care. Thank you for reading *Handle with Care: Managing Difficult Situations in Schools with Dignity and Respect* and sharing your thoughts. We hope this book motivates and inspires educators at all levels to do whatever it takes to ensure a culture of excellence when it comes to managing difficult situations. If we can assist in any way with the work you are doing, please reach out to us at:

ConnectEDDPublishing (563) 447-5776
or **info@connecteddpublishing.com**

Please also share your thoughts, along with the work you are doing related to this book, via social media using the hashtag #HandleWith-CareEDU Thank you for your dedication and commitment to excellence and to the students you serve.

CHAPTER 1

Would You Rather
I Call Mom or Dad?

J ack was a junior in high school. Like many teens, he didn't much care for school or the school rules and cared even less when he didn't understand them. Jack seemed indifferent about the referral sent to the office about him. The principal opened up the referral so they could look at it together; Jack remained disinterested. The referral indicated that Jack is continuously late to class and when he does arrive, he doesn't stay on task. Jack suddenly displayed some interest in the conversation, primarily to object to the content of the referral. "That's a bunch of crap. That's not true. Just give me my punishment and get me out of here," Jack countered. He was done and, at that point, everything was falling on deaf ears. The principal leaned in to pick up the phone and said, "Would you rather I call mom or dad?" Without total recall of every part of that conversation, the following

*was seared into the principal's mind. "Neither. You can't call my parents."
The principal replied, "Why not?"*

*"Because my dad shot and killed my mom and then killed himself. I live
with my aunt and uncle."*

*Jack explained that his dad shot and killed his mom and then turned
the gun on himself. The principal was stunned. After Jack left, the principal
immediately grabbed Jack's cumulative school folder. As a kindergartner,
Jack was described by his teachers as vibrant, smart, and sweet. As the years
progressed, he became quieter, withdrawn, and preoccupied because of his
"parents impending divorce." Then came 6th grade. Jack's folder contained
notes of concern about his peer interactions and decline in academic achievement followed by newspaper clippings detailing the tragedy Jack had shared.*

Hearing stories like this make you wonder how many other "Jacks"
are walking around schools carrying pain, worry, grief, and anxiety.
Granted, Jack's situation is extreme, but It should give us pause to
recognize children throughout the country are dealing with a lot of
pain and personal challenges. Some have fractured families, deceased
parents, incarcerated or drug-dependent parents or guardians, food
insecurity, and concerns for personal safety. Other children are living
with mental health issues, including depression and anxiety. Still others
feel alone and isolated. One thing for sure is that school may be the
only soft place to land for many students. One premise of *Culturize* is
that every educator is called to be a champion for every student, every
day. Whatever it takes. We are called to care about every student and
their circumstances by challenging the status quo. As champions for
students, we are responsible for creating schools and experiences that
learners both need and deserve. Every educator can relate to good days,
bad days, and days that just kick your tail. Regardless, every word and
deed either adds positively to the school culture or it doesn't. It's that
simple.

Throughout this book, the principles from *Culturize* are reviewed and applied to other scenarios so educators can positively impact school areas such as discipline, student activities, and school pride. Healthy and vibrant school cultures happen through positive relationships, clear expectations, boundaries, candid conversations, and empathy.

Baseline Assumptions

One of the most challenging facets of education is managing student discipline in a way that corrects behavior while simultaneously strengthening the school culture. The traditional, top-down, "Because I said so" approach to discipline or any type of decision-making is neither respectful nor effective. Engaging students and staff in conversations about more than just a student's conduct are essential to uncovering the feelings that may be influencing the behaviors. So what can we learn from Jack's story? What baseline assumptions can educators make to help them become more effective leaders?

- ◆ **Assumption #1** *You can assume that every student you come into contact with has, at some point in their life, had some level of trauma, pain, or personal challenge.* While Jack's story is extraordinarily traumatic, other students experience trauma in the form of neglect, abandonment, or verbal, physical, or sexual abuse. They witness violence in the home, drug and alcohol dependency, and many are surrounded by adults with serious mental health issues. Other students may be carrying the pain of being separated from a parent or sibling, either through a divorce, a court order, or even death. You can be sure many students are navigating the challenge that comes from living in poverty, food insecurity, and homelessness. Whatever the circumstances, far too many children are living in situations that are unhealthy and oftentimes unpredictable. A failure to recognize or acknowledge the suffering and turmoil others experience negatively impacts the relationships between students and staff, among staff members, and among students. Hearing Jack's story put an end to the question, "Would you rather I call mom or dad?" It is important to be mindful that every student's family structure and dynamic is unique, special, and ought to be validated. When needing to contact a parent now, the question to the student is, "Who else lives with you?" Responses range from mom or dad, mom and dad, stepmom and dad, to grandma and grandpa, my cousins, both of my moms, my dads, and everything in between. On more than one occasion students have responded, "My great grandparents." When we take the time to ask our students who else lives with them, we can learn a lot about their life outside of school. A grandparent may now live with the student because they are taking care of the student's parent who is ill. Those cousins who live with the student? They are doubled up in housing because the relatives fled the larger city violence to ensure the safety of their family. When we know this information, we can proactively put supports in place to help students overcome barriers that interfere with school attendance or performance.

+ **Assumption #2** *Outward expressions don't always align with internal feelings.* When we are attuned to the emotional cues of a student, we may better understand the function behind the behavior. At times school leaders, teachers, and parents/guardians assume too much about why a young person is responding the way they are. Simply asking, "Can you please help me understand why you seem (mad, sad, angry, nervous)?" signals that you have not predetermined or judged their behavior and also opens the conversation to more meaningful dialogue while also helping them develop an emotional vocabulary. In this way, adults can help students develop greater self-awareness which ultimately will impact their ability to better manage their thoughts, feelings, and behaviors. Thoughts influence feelings and feelings influence behaviors. Helping others recognize their thought patterns (negative, obsessive, worrisome) and developing ways to disrupt those patterns will prevent negative feelings and consequently, negative behaviors. It is important to respect the boundaries students establish in terms of what they are willing to share. When navigating a delicate situation, consider proactively saying to the student, "I am going to ask you some questions to better understand this situation, but you have every right

> Student outward expressions don't always align with their internal feelings.

and freedom to tell me you don't want to answer any questions you don't feel comfortable answering. I will honor that and will not press you on it. I would just ask that you please not lie to me." Students are more likely to respond thoughtfully and honestly when they have a choice and they know their voice is the most important one in the conversation. Student outward expressions don't always align with their internal feelings.

- **Assumption #3** *Adults don't always get it right.* How many times have we worked with students about their behavior only to recognize that other adults need to work on their self-management as well? Consider the scenario: A student is sent to the office. The ensuing referral indicates the student "F bombed" the teacher. At face value, that is troubling and completely inappropriate behavior from the student. Upon further questioning, the student reveals that he did F-bomb the teacher. The administrator asks the follow-up question "Can you help me understand why you spoke to the teacher that way?" The student explains that when he arrived late, the teacher announced *in front of the class,* "Not a big surprise that you are late again." A short time later the teacher was collecting homework assignments and loudly asked the student, "I don't suppose you have the assignment for me, do you?" Finally, as the students broke into a working group assignment, the teacher asked the student if there was "any chance" he brought a pencil today. In this scenario, whose behavior needs to be checked? Both the student and the teacher need to be addressed. No student should ever speak to a staff member that way. It is disrespectful, unwarranted, and does not do a single thing to help that student feel any better about himself. Yes, the short-term gratification of F-bombing the teacher may sit well, but long-term, such behavior is not positive and often does not reflect the heart or character of the student. There also needs to be a conversation with the teacher. Imagine if the teacher had greeted the tardy student with, "I'm happy to see you today." Is there any chance the student would have started to simmer over that greeting? If the teacher had privately said to the student, "Would you be able to give me the assignment tomorrow?" Or how would the student respond to a pencil simply being placed on his desk by the teacher? We agree and understand: the student was wrong; however, the student didn't lead with F-bombing the teacher. The student started to simmer and with each passing teacher dig, he percolated some more. Like a tea kettle, his ability to contain himself had reached a boiling point. The teacher was also wrong and, as the adult in the situation, had a responsibility to approach the student differently. As school leaders and colleagues, what sort of conversation are we willing to have with the teacher? It takes very little effort to point out to an adult where they had an opportunity to turn the situation into something more positive for both the student and the teacher. Asking teachers, "What prompted you to approach that student the way you did?" helps the teacher reflect and reframe situations with students. As evidenced by the digs at the student, the teacher has been frustrated with how the student has been managing his responsibilities in the class. Leaders help teachers reflect on their behavior, motivations, and emotions so the adult gains more self-awareness for similar situations in the future.

♦ **Assumption #4** *Assume the best about the intentions of students, colleagues, and people who report to you and extend them grace, especially when they have a misstep.* After COVID-19 hit, *grace* became more than just a word. *Grace* became a lifestyle and in many ways fundamentally altered what was deemed "important." Teachers and students gave each other wider latitude to navigate the unpredictable challenges that came with a worldwide pandemic. Although the political and societal landscapes have been fairly acrimonious recently, we must remember that most individuals are good people who innately want to do well, be respectful, and be viewed favorably by others. Despite the mistakes we make, when allowed the opportunity to rectify situations or behaviors, people are generally willing to do so--but not if they feel backed into a corner. If teachers, coaches, directors, or leaders believe the only path forward from a situation is dependent on the student or staff member admitting their faults and issuing some forced apology, any grace that may have existed will disappear. Consider this scenario:

> *A student is sent out of class for being disruptive and disrespectful, according to the teacher. You learn from the student that he feels the teacher targets him and when the teacher gets disrespectful with him, the student becomes disrespectful right back. As you talk through the situation, you can show him where he had a couple of opportunities to de-escalate the situation and likely could have remained in the class. Now less agitated, the student*

recognizes he didn't have to talk disrespectfully to the teacher. As you try to close the conference with the student you say, "How do you want to try and fix this situation?" He immediately and firmly states, "I am not apologizing to him."

Forcing students to apologize to someone else is ill-advised, for many reasons. First, many students have never been taught *how* to apologize, so they are very uncomfortable being in what is a foreign situation for them. Second, forcing a student to apologize takes away from their ability to hold themselves accountable for their words and actions. Finally, when you force a student to apologize to someone else, it likely will be delivered in the same way the apology came about-- forced. This does not, however, mean there shouldn't be an effort made to model for the student how to navigate this situation and move forward in the following way:

> *I understand you don't want to apologize. I'm not asking you to do that. You have identified points in the situation where you could have gone in a different direction. You also believe the teacher had those same opportunities. How comfortable would you be registering that with the teacher and having this conversation: "I want you to know that I got upset with you because I felt you were treating me disrespectfully. I don't know if that was your intent, but that's how I felt. I should not have spoken to you the way I did and can understand that you feel I was disrespectful to you. That won't happen again and I would like us to get a fresh start from here and move on."*

Students almost always agree to go back and talk to the teacher because they get to register how they felt but don't have to say, "I'm sorry." In our capacity as leaders, we can support students simply by helping them find acceptable language to explain the way they feel. In this scenario, the student is, in essence, apologizing but not forced to do so. Many adults and students do not know how to apologize, how to accept an apology or see the personal benefits of offering and receiving apologies.

The Four Agreements by Don Miguel Ruiz (1997) is a quick, insightful read about the four agreements Ruiz says we should make with ourselves about the way we want to live our lives. The third agreement states simply, "Don't make assumptions." Ruiz explains that we have a tendency to make assumptions about everything and we tend to believe our assumptions are the truth. Ruiz argues that assumptions often happen because we have agreed that it is not safe to ask questions or that others should know what we are thinking or feeling. As a result, we tend to make up a story in our mind about the thoughts or opinions others have of us, the decisions we make, or the motives behind our actions. Being clear about what we are doing and why we are doing it prevents widespread assumptions. It doesn't prevent all assumptions, as some will still make them because they either do not understand what is being said or they do not believe what they are being told. Whether you are a teacher, principal, parent, or partner, making assumptions often interferes with the quality and health of relationships. When we interact with students daily, regardless of their age, where do we need to check our assumptions? How do we help them check their presumptions about us or each other?

Don't Believe Everything You Think

Girl, you need to get on out of your head
And into your heart instead
Like I said
Don't believe everything you think.
From the song, "Don't Believe Everything You Think"
(Brice, Collins, Stone, 2012).

Our thoughts are rarely ever our own. They are influenced by personal experiences, family, friends, colleagues, relationships, social media, and even the daily news. Our beliefs about politics, religion, and social justice issues are often influenced by a myriad of sources.

> People often make decisions and take action based on feelings rather than facts.

Recognizing how thoughts influence feelings is important. Take, for example, a parent who is worried about their daughter because it is well past her curfew and she has yet to come home. The range of thoughts (she is past her curfew and there is going to be a conversation about this) changes the way the mother feels and acts (still hasn't heard from daughter, has texted her, called her, started calling her friends, and ready to call the police). What starts as a concern that her daughter didn't meet expectations by missing her curfew shifts to an all-out panic-stricken fear that her daughter is in danger or worse. This range of thoughts and feelings can happen in a very short amount of time. How else do your thoughts create internal feelings? For example, consider your thin friend who constantly talks about how fat she is or the 4.0 student who insists he is going to fail his next exam. While the feelings may be valid, we can see the thin girl right in front of us, and from what we know about the studious one, it's not likely he will fail anything. Despite evidence to the contrary, the thin one and the student believe otherwise. Their thought patterns have impacted how they feel and the assumptions made. People often make decisions and take action based on feelings rather than facts.

This takes us back to the third agreement from *The Four Agreements*: don't make assumptions. Things simply are not always as they appear and what we think may not always be accurate. A middle school principal shared this situation:

I had a student who recently lost it on one of my teachers over his cell phone being taken away. Tom had been asked three times by the teacher to put his phone away before she took it from him. At the end of class, the teacher told him he would have to retrieve it from the main office at the end of the day. Tom became argumentative; the teacher remained calm. Rather than accept the outcome, Tom lashed out at the teacher and, as he walked away, muttered, "Fucking bitch." When the situation was brought to me, I found myself having an emotional reaction--it was anger. I don't tolerate students speaking to staff that way and, frankly, I was appalled. In my head, I immediately went to how I was going to punish Tom. I thought about how important it was to send a message to Tom and all students that this was not acceptable. I also knew my staff would be observing and responding to whatever action I took.

Tom was brought to my office. I asked him what he said to the teacher. He denied saying anything to her. When I stated that I was told he referred to her in a vulgar way, he denied that. "I said I hate this school. That's all I said." When I asked him what would motivate the teacher to report this, he responded, "Because she hates me. Everybody hates me." He then dissolved into heaping sobs and pulled his hood up over his head and face. I asked Tom what evidence he had that "everybody" hated him. He talked in circles a bit and could not provide a single, specific example. No one hated him, but he had convinced himself that others did. I told Tom we needed to work through some of his perceptions and connect him with people who could help him sort through his feelings. I softly said to him, "To move forward, Tom, I need you to be a young man of integrity and truthfully tell me what happened in that class." Tom responded, "I said that to her. It's true. I'm sorry. I was just so mad."

After driving Tom home, I called the teacher and apologized for the disrespect she experienced from Tom. I explained to her that it is clear that he is hurting and needs our help. I asked her if she would be willing to meet with Tom and me after he returned from his suspension. She graciously agreed and said she was willing to help him.

What this principal did in this story was essential to helping Tom transition from anger and despair to hope and acceptance of the help being offered. While the principal stated he initially wanted to lead with punishment, the way he spoke to and questioned Tom made it possible for Tom to tell the truth while also seeking to better understand what motivated him to speak to the teacher the way he had. What could have whirled around in the teacher's lounge was simply that a student called a teacher an "F-ing bitch." End of story. Instead, by reaching out to the teacher in this situation, the principal modeled compassion for what she experienced but also enlisted compassion for Tom's circumstances. The situation provided an opportunity for Tom to challenge the assumptions he was making about how others thought of him. He believed everyone "hated" him. The teacher and the principal both quashed that assumption and they did so with care and compassion. In this scenario, the principal was a champion for the student...and the teacher.

Taking Care of Those In Your Charge

The premise of *Culturize: Every Student. Every Day. Whatever it Takes.* is that we must expect all staff to champion for all students. Teachers and leaders who transform their belief systems and focus on what is best for kids make an indelible mark on a school. By creating a culture of excellence, carrying the banner for their students and school, and serving as merchants of hope, school and teacher leaders are never deterred by failure or the unknown. These forward-thinking educators remain motivated by hope and faith. They turn that motivation into action in ways that inspire others to do the same.

It's no mystery that student learn better from people they believe care about them. As such, high-functioning schools rightly focus on developing supportive and authentic relationships with students. Those teachers and leaders who make relationships with their students the cornerstone of their commitment reap tremendous professional and personal rewards. When we commit to knowing our students personally, we are saying to them, "I see you. I value you. I am here for you." They know it. They feel it. They need it. Adults are no different. We must also work to strengthen and deepen the relationships we have with colleagues, supervisors, and those who report to us.

> When we commit to knowing our students personally, we are saying to them, "I see you. I value you. I am here for you."

With all the demands placed on teachers and administrators daily, it is no wonder that taking care of adults has been left to chance. One of the greatest challenges in school settings is the "us" vs "them" mentality with "us" being teachers and other staff and "them" being administrators. Some of this delineation is a natural by-product of duties and contracts. Most school administrators have served as classroom teachers but must then learn how to execute administrative duties in service and support of the job they once did as classroom teachers. It's always intriguing when people say, "You're a principal? I would never want that job." As accountability measures for educators continue to rise, and the resources to meet those expectations decline, there can be natural angst. Both teachers and leaders often work far too many hours, don't get the adequate sleep and necessary rest, struggle to meet self-care goals including exercise and nutrition, and, at times, place personal relationships on the back burner in service of caring for and guiding other peoples' children. The current trend is to glorify busyness even if it wreaks havoc on our health, our personal and professional relationships, and our sense of order. The last thing our profession needs is to pit teachers against administrators and vice versa. Each serves a unique and critical role in a school system. When adults struggle to connect with other professionals, regardless of job title, that tension is often the result of two things: people don't trust one another and people don't feel valued. If educators are to be champions for all students, we must also be advocates for and support one another as well.

Schools must be a safe environment for students, staff, and administration. In the era of school lockouts, lock-ins, and lockdowns, we tend to lose sight of emotional safety in exchange for an emphasis on physical safety. Take active shooter drills, for example. While it is essential to plan and prepare for an armed intruder, we must try to separate the *possibility* of a school shooting from the *probability* of such an event. Across the country schools prepare for armed intruder events through drills, announcements, and training—and rightly so. Equally important is preparing for and adequately responding to staff who are under emotional duress as a result of the growing and intensive demands of the education profession.

When the pandemic hit, school leaders were right to assess the emotional health of students. Did we also consider how to keep a pulse on staff well-being?

Although administrators certainly must provide care for their staff, that cannot serve as a substitute for the support that staff members can provide to one another. Schools have long been staples of congeniality. We greet each other at the coffee pot, ask how the weekend was, and wish each other a good day. While these are appropriate forms of interaction, they should serve as a starting point of our interactions, yet they frequently serve as the endpoint. We often don't go beyond the surface, and, as a result, we don't *genuinely* get to know and understand one another. *Culturize* calls for every child to have the opportunity to be a part of something great. How can we intentionally ensure that every adult has the opportunity to be a part of something great?

Note to Readers: To close out each section for the remainder of the book, we will offer an *Eyes on Culture in Action* segment designed to provide practical suggestions and ideas to assist you in identifying areas in your school that would benefit from implementing the four (4) core principles from *Culturize:* Champion for Students, Expect Excellence, Carry the Banner, and Be a Merchant of Hope.

EYES ON CULTURE IN ACTION

Handwritten notes to staff: While this is a small gesture, it is always meaningful to the recipient. Committing to writing five personal notes a week to staff members enables school leaders to demonstrate appreciation while also acknowledging what those staff members offer and why they were hired.

Provide time for students to do the same: November is a great month to give students time during school to write a note of gratitude to any staff member they choose. This makes both students and staff feel a part of something great. It's always interesting who the students identify as someone they want to thank—teachers, coaches, school counselors, and administrators are conventional recipients, but the number of cards submitted for secretaries, kitchen staff, security staff, and custodians is equally impressive. Gestures—small and grand—can create this sense of community, belonging, and connectedness.

Calling parents/significant others of staff members: No one ever tires of hearing positive things about their children, no matter how old they are. Making a few phone calls to parents/partners and telling them how valuable their family member is to the organization is a great way to remind staff that they are a part of something great.

Honor a staff member every week: Taking time to celebrate the contributions staff members make and allowing anyone in the school to nominate a staff member for recognition, strengthens a school community. Prepare to be surprised by the number of students who nominate a staff member who may not even be their teacher. School leaders can go to a classroom or office each week and simply read what the nominator wrote about a staff member. Provide a traveling trophy, mini school mascot, or a poster about your school values to the recognized employee to keep in their room or office for the week. Honoring the employee in front of students is important. It reminds students how special the adults are in their school and validates traits such as commitment, generosity, tenacity, and kindness.

Use social media to celebrate the great things going on in your school: Take time to walk through classrooms, videotape classroom lessons or student activities, and post them on social media—always with a note of gratitude to the staff member showcased in the videos.

Provide a wellness room for staff: The level of stress many adults are carrying is unhealthy and negatively impacts their performance and their relationships. Providing space and encouraging staff to walk the building or use the exercise equipment before or after school and during their prep or lunchtime signals that staff health and well-being matters to school leaders.

Create a calming room for staff: If possible, provide staff a small room away from their classroom or office that has a spa-like feel to it—relaxing music, comfortable furniture, coffee/tea, tranquil lighting, etc.

Providing space for staff to take even just a few minutes to experience some peace will reap benefits.

As mentioned earlier, supportive and meaningful relationships are often rooted in **trust**. In her book, *Rising Strong*, Brene Brown (2015) uses an acronym that she created to explain the elements of what she calls, "the anatomy of trust." The acronym is **BRAVING** and the elements are:

+ Boundaries: You accept the boundaries others set and you are willing to set limits with others.
+ Reliability: You do what you say you are going to do. Your integrity is such that you do not overpromise and underdeliver.
+ Accountability: You hold yourself accountable by acknowledging your mistakes, apologizing for them, and changing your behavior.
+ Vault: You hold the confidences of others and do not share any news that is not yours to share.
+ Integrity: You lead with courage and honesty, even when it is uncomfortable or unpopular.
+ Non-judgment: You can be fully present in a peaceful manner and refrain from judging others or yourself.
+ Generosity: You extend empathetic compassion and assume the best about the intentions, words, and behaviors of others. You lead with grace toward others.

Lack of trust among the adults in a school community kills any existing positive culture. As an educator, which of the **BRAVING** elements are strengths for you? Which ones are a struggle for you? Cultivating trust in working relationships is essential to finding joy in our work and elevating our impact. In *Culturize*, the following questions are provided to determine if students could trust staff:

+ Are you honest with your students?
+ Are you dependable in following through when you promise to do something?
+ Are you available when you say you will be?
+ Do you demonstrate a sense of empathy when students hesitate to do what you ask or fail to follow through on what you agreed upon?
+ Do you take time to ask questions when students let you down rather than make assumptions regarding the reasons why?
+ Are you impeccable with your word? (2017, p. 36)

Now, go back to each of these questions and insert colleagues and/ or staff where the word "students" appears. (No, really go back to the questions at this point).

If we are to truly take care of those in our charge, we must be able to say "yes" to these questions when it comes to our students, our colleagues, and those who report to us. To take this a step further, ask yourself this question: How do I show up for my students, colleagues, and staff? Attending events, supporting individual efforts in and out of the classroom, and offering public praise for a job well done should be the norm, the baseline. How do we show up for others in good times? And bad? One educator shared how strongly she feels about showing up in bad times. She is faithful about attending the visitation or funerals for the loved ones of her colleagues and her students. She explains:

The death of a loved one is one of the most painful times in a person's life. When I attended the funeral for the father of a student after he was killed in a motorcycle accident, she never forgot it. During winter break, I found out a student's grandmother died unexpectedly. I knew he was raised by his grandma and this was a major loss for him. I went to her funeral and he kept saying to me, "I can't believe you came. I really appreciate it." When I sat with a colleague at Hospice when her husband died, she never forgot it. We have to be willing to show up for others in joy and sorrow. There is no better way to say, "I care."

Imagine (and celebrate) a school culture in which all adults feel this way—a school where all staff members are "all-in" for their colleagues and their students during the important events of their lives. A principal friend shared this experience:

It was late afternoon on the Friday before going into spring break. The office phone was ringing after the office had closed. I was sitting in my office trying to knock out some things on my to-do list before leaving for the break. The phone rang a second time and although I wanted to ignore it, I got up out of my office chair and went to the front desk, and answered the phone. On the other end was the local Hospice House calling to let me know that the father of one of my students was there and likely only had a few days to live. My heart sank. The voice on the other end wondered if there was any chance the student's diploma had arrived yet so his dad could see it before he died.

The principal who shared this did so as he discussed how significant the school community can be in the lives of students, staff, and families. The fact that the family reached out to the school in their time of need signaled that the culture of that school was what that family needed at that time. *Culturize* is defined as "cultivating a community of learners by behaving in a kind, caring, honest, and compassionate manner in order to challenge and inspire each member of the school community to become more than they ever thought possible" (Casas, 2017, p. 4). This is the call; this is the challenge. Teachers and leaders throughout the country are doing whatever it takes to reach every student, every day.

19

EYES ON CULTURE IN ACTION

Show up: Attend events, ask questions, *truly* listen, follow up, provide assurance, be empathetic, be joyful for others in good times, and empathetic with them in bad. When we show up for others with this spirit, a culture of trust grows and deepens.

Be a gatekeeper: Have the ability and integrity to keep private, personal information confidential. Understand what is your news to share with others and what is not. From something as simple as waiting to announce a staff member's pregnancy until permitted to do so, to remaining silent when the drunk driving arrest of a staff member's child hits the newspaper, even though you have already known. When people in your charge tell you about their complicated pregnancy, their parent's terminal diagnosis, that their marriage is on the brink or that their child scored a perfect ACT, that sharing is rooted in trust. Conduct yourself in a way that makes others think they are the only one who has talked to you in confidence.

Be reliable: Do what you say you are going to do. Be where you say you will be. Say what you mean; mean what you say. And where you fall short—because we all do—own it by apologizing and committing to do better.

Withhold judgment: We all know the saying, "If you don't have anything nice to say, don't say anything at all." While this certainly is the path we should all follow, the saying, "If you don't have anything nice to say, come sit by me" is more often the reality. It is human nature to make judgments—we all do it. We judge how other people talk, what they wear, how they treat others. We make these judgments in our minds and sometimes say them out loud. Have you ever been on the receiving end of the ruthless judgment of someone else? It hurts. It makes us feel misunderstood and diminishes our sense of self. The next time you find yourself judging someone, ask yourself if you have enough information to make that judgment. Withholding judgment is essential to cultivating trusting relationships among the adults and with the students.

That Was Not My Intention (But What Was the Effect?)

A former principal shared this story:

> I was in my 9th year as a principal and my 15th year as an educator. I received a phone call at home on a Saturday morning. On the other end was a former student that I had in class my second year of teaching. After the initial shock, surprise, and thrill to hear from Chad, he shared why he was calling me after all these years. He was going through the 12 steps of Alcoholics Anonymous as part of his sobriety plan. He was on step 8—**made a list of all persons we had harmed and became willing to make amends to them all.** I was immediately taken back to the year Chad was my student. He was harsh, dismissive, and seemed angry. Chad offered he had been an alcoholic, even in high school. He spent many years being drunk, angry, and bitter. So why was he calling me? Chad said that he appreciated that I always treated him fairly, encouraged him, and cared about him. Then he said, "You may not remember this, but you kept me after class one day and told me when I decided to stop being angry and get out of my way, then, and only then, would I experience the kind of happiness I deserved. Those words stayed with me and I have finally stopped being angry and I am just now learning that I do deserve to be happy. I was not very nice to you, but you never held it against me. I just wanted to tell you I am sorry for that and to let you know how your words inspired me." I was stunned

and giddy at the same time. I thanked him for his call and told him these are the kinds of phone calls that keep educators going. I remember feeling excited about telling my family and close friends about this amazing phone call. As I replayed that conversation in my mind, I went back to what Chad said: "Those words stayed with me." I was joyful that my words had a positive impact on Chad's life, even if I didn't remember saying them. I immediately started thinking about times I may have said something hurtful or dispiriting without even realizing it. If the positive, uplifting words I spoke to Chad were forgotten by me, were there times that I used hurtful, dismissive words that had an unintended negative impact on someone else? It was a good reminder about how important it is to be intentional with my words.

Being cognizant of the impact we can and do have on students, colleagues, and those we supervise is essential to the way we can influence the experiences others have in our schools. In *Culturize*, readers are asked to reflect on the following questions regarding the kind of influence you have on your school and in your classroom:

+ Do your words inspire others for success or shame?
+ Do your actions result in wellness or weariness? (Casas, 2017, p.9)

So does someone's motive or intention matter more than their actions or effect? Intentions are important to consider, but actions are what shape our relationships and school cultures. We can be defined by the people we are known to surround ourselves with, the beliefs we express, and the way we treat others. When we surround ourselves with people who **act** in the best interest of others, we increase the odds that our actions are more impactful.

The impact of our words and actions can place great weight on others—positively or negatively. How often have you been on the receiving end of someone else's comments or actions that have either hurt your feelings or angered you? We have all had this experience and if we are brave enough to have an honest conversation with the other person and report our hurt or anger, be prepared for the, "I didn't mean it like that" response or, "I didn't intend to hurt your feelings." Granted, we would feel much better knowing the hurt wasn't intentional, but does that entirely remove the sting? Not likely.

How many times have we witnessed a public figure issue an apology that goes like this: "I'm sorry if you were offended by what I said (or did), but that was not my intent."? This is an excellent example of how to issue a useless apology. *"I'm sorry if you were offended…."* is the equivalent of, *"I didn't do anything wrong; you just took it the wrong way."* This type of apology includes no accountability and invalidates the feelings of the other person(s). Most people do not know how to issue a genuine apology (e.g., "I am sorry for the pain I have caused you."). Even more, people do not know how to accept one (e.g., "Oh, that's OK." No, it is not.). There is an underlying reason people cannot issue a genuine apology and exhibit a willingness to accept an inadequate apology. Take a couple of minutes to write down the name(s) of the person(s) who come to mind when you read the following questions:

1. Who has modeled to you what it means to be a high-character person?
2. Who has demonstrated for you how to love unconditionally?
3. Who best exemplifies commitment—the person who won't ever let others down?
4. Who has been a pillar of strength—someone you know who can and will get through any challenge presented?

5. Who has modeled hope to you—the person who sees the sun in any storm and provides reassurance that you will be okay no matter what?

6. Who has modeled forgiveness to you?

Whenever anyone does this exercise, they usually sail through the first five questions but invariably either struggle to answer or need more time to write a name for the question on forgiveness. It is not uncommon, but it is unfortunate. It speaks to the fact that forgiveness is not often given serious consideration and people don't have meaningful experiences around forgiveness. The reason people have difficulty extending and receiving an apology is simply that it has not been modeled to them.

A teacher enrolled in graduate school for educational leadership relayed this experience:

I was shadowing an administrator in my building as part of my practicum hours. She let me observe her every interaction so long as the other party (student, teacher, or parent) agreed to let me participate. In one instance, a science teacher had come to the principal steaming that a freshman student in his class had been disrespectful. The teacher tried to redirect the student and get him to engage with the lab but the student became more disrespectful toward the teacher and caused a scene in the class. When the teacher told him he wanted him to get on task, he responded, "Do you think I care about what you want? Do you think anybody in this class ever cares what you think?"

Within minutes, the student was standing at the principal's door. He knew why he was summoned and his armor was on full display. His arms were folded, his jaw was clenched, and he was argumentative. He admitted to his behavior and accepted his consequence.

The principal asked the student how he wanted to repair things with the teacher. He said he didn't know how, but that he wasn't going to apologize. The principal then said, "What if you considered going to the teacher and saying this: 'I want you to know that I realize how out of line and disrespectful I was to you. I am dealing with some personal stuff and let it get to me too much. I would like to come back to class and I can promise you nothing like that will happen again.' The principal looked right at him and said, "Do you know what you wouldn't be saying?" He answered, "I'm sorry."

If we have any intention of maintaining positive, healthy, and loving relationships, we must acknowledge when we have behaved in hurtful ways. We must be willing to forgive—often and quickly. For some students, the school may be the only place where they learn about forgiveness. Adults must model this, but sometimes we get so entrenched in our feelings and experiences that it's hard to recognize the need of others at that moment. We also need to assess our role in escalating or de-escalating situations. We have all encountered people who have to be right **and** have the last word (a brutal combination, by the way). Some students marinate in environments like this outside of school. Helping students find their voice and validating their feelings may be the only chance they have to cultivate skills and close the gap between intent and impact.

EYES ON CULTURE IN ACTION

Listen to the emotion more than the words: When a student is yelling, crying, and saying inappropriate things, focus on the emotion. Too often people are listening only to the words for the purpose of placing blame or fault rather than responding to the hurt and pain.

Listen to understand: Most of us are wired to listen for the purpose of responding and not to truly understand the perspective of others. Remove the point/counterpoint tone contentious conversations can take, especially when people are hurting. Listening to understand will yield a quicker and healthier resolution to the matter.

Offer a safe space: Be the type of educator/friend/parent/partner that creates conditions for others to candidly talk through things without feeling judged. When people can talk plainly without filtering, they feel safer about being candid to achieve clarity. That candor can illuminate how the other person is processing information and experiences.

Model how to apologize: There are three key ingredients to an effective apology (and, "I'm sorry if you were offended" is not one of them). Issuing an apology requires saying, "I'm sorry," acknowledging the hurt caused and the impact on the other person, and a commitment to do better moving forward. Say, for example, that you repeated to another colleague something a different colleague shared with you in confidence and it got back to him. A healthy apology sounds like this: "I am sorry I violated your confidence by repeating what you told me in confidence. It was inappropriate and insensitive of me and I hurt you and hurt the trusting relationship we have with one another. I have learned from this and recognize that sometimes I like to feel important by letting people know that I am a person others come to. It was wrong of me and I will not let it happen again. I am sorry." This apology is direct and sincere. Rather than blaming others it assumes responsibility and signals a commitment to do better in the future. Imagine if we modeled this type of apology to students when possible and warranted.

Offer a path forward through forgiveness: Have you ever been in a situation where one person offended another? Take the scenario above where one colleague violated the trust of another by sharing confidential information. More often than not, the injured party usually responds to the "I'm sorry" with "It's OK." Was it OK that the colleague repeated private information? No. Is it OK when a student spreads a rumor about another student? No. So why is the automatic response usually, "It's OK"? Because people don't generally know how to accept an apology. Imagine if the injured party instead responded in the following way: "I appreciate the apology. I have been very hurt by this because I felt I could trust you. I have felt hurt and betrayed and I don't want to feel this way. I accept your apology and ask that you please not violate my trust again. I value you and your friendship and hopefully we both learn from this so we are better friends to one another going forward." The standard response, "It's OK" dismisses the seriousness of the offense and lessens the likelihood of changed behavior. By revealing how the injured party felt, the offender has better insight into the extent of the hurt caused.

Behaviors are Seen, But Often Misunderstood

In his book, *Talking to Strangers (2019)*, Malcolm Gladwell shines a light on human behavior and interpersonal relationships. Gladwell suggests that there is often a "mismatch" in the outward expressions of emotions and the internal feelings people have. He cites the Amanda Knox case as a prime example. Knox was an American foreign exchange student convicted in an Italian court for the 2007 murder of her British student exchange roommate, Meredith Kercher. The Italian press dubbed Knox "Foxy Knoxy." In the video footage, Knox can be seen outside the crime scene, smiling, hugging, and kissing her boyfriend. Gladwell argues because Knox did not present a trace of hysteria, trauma, or grief, people jumped to the conclusion that she must have committed the murder, even though they had no idea how Knox was feeling internally. While Gladwell's theory has been challenged by many, we do find it applicable to the experience teachers and leaders can have with students and colleagues. Take the earlier story about Tom, the student whose phone was taken away by his teacher, resulting in him launching expletives at her. From the outside, Tom presented as a hostile, entitled, defiant young man who simply wanted his phone back. The flood of tears and subsequent breakdown revealed a deeper, more broken-hearted story than the surface version of a student launching profanity.

This "mismatch" often presents itself when school officials need to interact with upset parents, a scenario some educators try to avoid. They struggle to make the parent phone call or schedule that face-to-face meeting because of an internal fear that the conversation won't go well. Oddly, this has become particularly true for veteran teachers. Perhaps this is a result of the changing landscape in recent years. In not such a distant past, when a teacher called home it was the student who was questioned, quizzed, and on the defense. Many teachers have expressed dismay at how some parents/guardians now respond to their phone call by challenging the teacher on her teaching strategies, quizzing the teacher about his grading practices, and the often-mentioned, "My child feels like you don't like him." Coaching other staff members to work through these conversations can be challenging, but we must see the parents/guardians as partners in supporting and challenging students to realize their fullest potential. How can we do this?

Seek clarification: Ask open-ended, empathetic questions to gain a better understanding of the situation from the parent/guardian perspective. "I am calling to share an observation with you about (insert student name) and see if you can help me better understand how I can support her." This is likely going to result in a different response than if the conversation is led with, "Your child has three missing assignments and slept in class today. I don't know how to help her." By leading with statements that focus on negative behaviors, we invite more conflict and misunderstanding.

Provide a generous assessment: Most parents/guardians don't want to hear negative things about their children (even if it is true). How the information about a student is shared with their parent/guardian makes all the difference in the predicted response. Sometimes, to check off our to-do list, we hastily make phone calls and we run the risk of making proclamations rather than providing clarifications, which can promptly backfire. "I just wanted to give you a quick call and let you know that (insert student name) isn't taking care of her schoolwork and I have reminded her several times. She just doesn't seem to care." This approach is likely to put the parent/guardian on defense and interfere with their desire to cooperate. When seeking clarification, offer a generous assessment of their child. "I have the pleasure of working with (insert student name) every day and some of the things I appreciate about her is her willingness to learn something new, the way she includes other students, and her definite desire to do better. She is struggling in my class right now and I was wondering if you had any insight as to how I can help her?" One approach is more likely to result in the parent positively engaging with the teacher, yielding better results.

Healthy school environments encourage students to go to other adults and ask for what they need. Helping parents to view and experience their school as a safe and supportive environment for their children will help them encourage their children to advocate for themselves before parents intervene. It is appropriate and, at times, necessary for a parent to step in. Advocating need not be adversarial, though. Some parents may become caustic and verbally attack us. Being on the receiving end of this is disconcerting, but this is also the point at which the educator needs to proceed with caution.

If school officials become defensive or argumentative, the focus will shift to the behavior of that professional rather than the student. Might we extinguish this divisiveness by simply offering the following to a parent? "You not only have a right to advocate for your child, but you also have an obligation to do so." This simple statement says, "I'm not threatened by your advocacy. We don't need to have a power struggle here. Let's work together to help your child." Advocating is identifying areas of concern or worry and raising the awareness of others that some need of the student is not being met. That is the duty of a parent and when school personnel embrace the parental right and responsibility to advocate, conversations become more positive and productive and less divisive and contentious:

> *A mother calls to tell you, the principal, that one of her child's high school teachers got into a political discussion in class and "basically told students who to vote for" in an upcoming election. The mother proceeded to say that her daughter, Emily, felt uncomfortable because she did not agree with the teacher and her daughter indicated she wasn't going to respond to questions in class anymore because Emily felt judged by the teacher. As is your practice, you ask if the student or parent have discussed this with the teacher. The mother says she did talk to the teacher but felt the teacher downplayed the situation. You tell the parent that you want to look into the matter and get back to her. After discussing the matter with the teacher, you learn that the teacher did reference the upcoming election and indicated that "some people" do think if you vote one way you are supporting policies that are harmful to minorities and the poor. You press the teacher on the "some people" comment asking if she can appreciate how the student felt that she, as the classroom teacher, was telling her how to vote. The teacher was apologetic. You ask the teacher what standard was being taught through that class discussion. There wasn't one—the discussion took on a life of its own and the teacher said she should have reigned it in. The teacher indicates she wants to apologize to Emily and her mom. You remind the teacher that she is too good of a teacher to have her reputation tarnished because she is perceived as being intolerant of*

the views others may have that differ from hers. She thanks you and apologizes for the situation she has put you in. You tell the teacher that the best resolution to this matter is to meet with Emily and her mom.

You follow up with Emily's mom and ask if they would be willing to meet with you and the teacher. She declines so you meet with Emily and her mom without the teacher. You share what you learned through your conversation with the teacher. You want to assure Emily and her mom that Emily had every right to raise the concern. You ask Emily if she had any concerns about returning to the class or worries as to how the teacher would treat her. She doesn't. Emily states to you and her mother that the teacher is really good; nothing like this has happened before and she has learned a lot from the teacher. You ask Emily if she feels the teacher cares about her and wants her to be successful. She agrees. You tell Emily's mom that the teacher is an effective teacher who cares about her students and feels badly that this was the result of the classroom discussion. You tell Emily's mom that there is value in having Emily meet with the teacher to talk through this situation so each can better understand the other and to repair the relationship. Emily's mom agrees to let you meet with Emily and the teacher.

This scenario reveals a couple of important things for educators to consider:

+ Adults don't always get it right and it is important to acknowledge that reality.
+ Student voice improves the overall experience for students and staff. Emily certainly felt better about her situation and likely helped the teacher reflect and do better for other students.
+ Strong relationships between home and school enable peaceful resolutions to conflicts. Because the principal was approachable

and the teacher was widely respected, even by Emily, the family and the school could work together to resolve the matter.

+ Educators can be held accountable for what they say and do without being thrown under the school bus in the process. The principal made a point to ask Emily about her feelings toward the teacher. Overall, her opinion of the teacher was highly favorable and it was helpful for her mother to hear that from Emily.

+ Involving students in the discussions with parents is an important element to resolving issues. While parents/guardians are concerned about the level of achievement their child is having in school, that pales in comparison to how they feel their child is treated by the adults in the school.

It is incumbent upon teachers and leaders to help parents/guardians recognize that their child's school is a safe, supportive, and ideal environment for their child to self-advocate before the parent intercedes. We must put systems and structures into place so the optimal conditions exist for students to do this safely and confidently.

EYES ON CULTURE IN ACTION

Set the stage early: Talk with parents/guardians about the culture your school promotes around parental advocacy and family involvement. Depending on the child's age, it is important to let parents/guardians know that classroom concerns should first be addressed with the classroom teacher. For early elementary-aged students, parents should be encouraged to include the child in the dialogue with the teacher. As children progress to upper elementary and older, they should be encouraged to first talk to the teacher themselves. When situations are not resolved at that level, it is appropriate for students to go to a school counselor and then to an administrator.

Encourage self-advocacy: When students come to the teacher, counselor, or administrator, they should be praised for bringing their concerns to the attention of adults. Encouraging student voice in the communication process is an education in itself. By celebrating students' voices, schools can glean more about the practices, policies, and procedures that may need a second look.

Coach staff to embrace parent/guardian input: Typically, teachers desire and expect some degree of perfectionism from themselves. When a student or parent/guardian registers displeasure, it's easy and natural to become defensive. School leaders need to spend time coaching staff members how to respond to student/parent criticism and concerns. Specifically, help staff to recognize defensive body language and tone (both voice and email) that signal to the parent/guardian that their input is being rejected rather than genuinely considered.

Support staff...even when they are wrong: There is a difference between supporting and defending staff when missteps take place. We can expect staff to mishandle situations from time to time—they are human, with their own sets of beliefs, emotions, and stress. Many dedicated, hard-working staff members feel a parent complaint is a referendum on their overall professionalism—it isn't and they need to hear that from the school leader.

CHAPTER 2

Core Principle 1:
Champion for Students - Culturizing Discipline

To create safe and optimal learning environments for all students, rules, consequences, and the logic behind disciplinary expectations are imperative to the order of a school setting and equally important to the culture of the larger community. At the heart of meaningful and effective school discipline are clarity, fairness, and consistency. Discipline should be viewed as an opportunity for educators to teach and for students to learn—and in some situations, for students to teach the educators, if we are willing to pause and listen. Students want to know that they matter. They want to know if they have a say about their experience and if what they have to say matters to the adults. How we connect with them and *truly listen* tells them what matters to us.

When addressing student discipline issues, it is essential to focus on student strengths and value and not just on their wrongdoing. Helping students recognize other choices they could have made is one part of the discussion. Equally important is helping them move forward, free of ridicule or judgment. Regardless of what the student has done--fighting, cheating, being disrespectful—they need to know you believe in them and that their mistake does not negatively define who they are or their value within the school community. It's important to close discipline conferences with something like the following:

You had a misstep here. It's just that. You will likely have others in the future, but perhaps you can learn from this situation and not repeat this type of mistake. I'm not mad at you and I'm not upset with you. I don't want you seeing me in the hallway and thinking that I am judging you for this. I'm not. I want to encourage you to file this under "experience" and move on. Can you do that for me? Can you do that for yourself?

And then be quiet. Get comfortable with the quiet between you. Sit with that child in silence. We don't need to overtalk and disrupt a student's ability to listen, process, and respond. Silence and wait time are important forms of communication. When children process what has just been said to them and the grace that has been extended, watch the bricks of shame and guilt fall off their shoulders. They will know and feel the care you have for them as a person and the unspoken fear they have in that situation will have been addressed. They will appreciate that you continue to think highly of them and that you are not judging them. They will understand you want them to learn from the experience and that you want them to move forward, burden-free.

Students frequently carry shame when they misbehave. They don't generally need someone to say to them, "You should be ashamed of yourself." They already hear that from a variety of sources and they feel it, even if it's unwarranted and unhealthy. We have a responsibility to help students develop and tap into an emotional vocabulary so they can identify and explain what they are feeling. Providing experiences and language for what they are feeling will interrupt that pattern of self-doubt, blame, guilt, and shame. Many children do not have models for healthy approaches to self-awareness and emotional regulation, but they can gain this through trusting connections with adults at their schools. To be a champion for all students requires being a champion for students with behavior issues, even when disciplinary action is warranted. Behind every successful student is an adult who served as a champion for that student:

Jamal was a sophomore doing absolutely nothing in English class. When he wasn't sleeping, he was off-task and disrupting the learning for students and the teacher's ability to teach. On this particular day, Jamal was sent to meet with the principal. Jamal gave every excuse as to why he wouldn't be successful in the English class. Jamal was lobbying to be dropped from the class, stating his behavior wasn't going to change. The principal looked up Jamal's assessments while he was sitting across the desk from him. Although Jamal was failing his English class miserably, Jamal scored at the 82nd percentile in his most recent reading assessment. Was Jamal bored in class? Was he simply refusing to use his abilities to be successful in English? Was he acting out for attention? Jamal conceded he wasn't going to do the work and the principal was wasting his time. The principal also knew the English teacher was beyond frustrated with Jamal and the disruptions he was making in her class. Without directly stating so, it was clear that the teacher did not want Jamal to continue in her class. The principal announced to Jamal that he would not be going back to the English class and that Jamal would be moving to Honors English. "I'm not going to Honors English," Jamal protested. "You can't make me do that. I won't do anything in that class." The principal said to Jamal, "You aren't doing anything now in general English. If you choose not to do anything, that's up to you, but you are going to do nothing among other students with whom you have the same capabilities."

A few weeks later, the principal called Jamal in to review his status in Honors English 10. He had an F grade. The principal drew 18 dash marks on the whiteboard in his office. He pointed out to Jamal that there were 18 weeks in the course. Jamal currently had an F. If Jamal failed this required course, he would have to take it again. The principal then drew 18 additional dash marks on the board to signify the possibility of Jamal having to retake the course. The principal said to Jamal, "So you are currently taking the 18-week course and getting an F. If you fail, you will have to take the course again. You are currently on schedule to take an 18-week course for 36-weeks. Help me understand how this makes sense, Jamal?"

The whiteboard illustration demonstrated a reality to Jamal, a reality in which far too many students find themselves. If we are truly going to be champions for students, we must look for alternative, and possibly unconventional, paths for students to experience success. The principal could have given Jamal detentions, held a conference with his parents/guardians and the classroom teacher, or could have simply withdrawn Jamal from the course. By looking deeper into the situation, Jamal ended up in an Honors track that would have previously seemed improbable. Rather than strictly focusing on discipline and punishment, the landscape for success can change in service of providing enriched opportunities for students, even ones they don't want. The principal's actions remind us that every student is one caring adult away from achieving greatness.

Set the Stage: Be Clear

At the core of every productive classroom or student opportunity is an environment that is rooted in trust, compassion, and clarity. At the center of every unpleasant (or even harmful) experience is distrust, callousness, and ambiguity. A classroom or school culture with clear expectations, combined with the outward expression of personal care and concern for others, sets the stage for the *prevention* of negative behaviors, not just *reacting* to them.

When one or two students have difficulty with self-management in a classroom, there are usually issues and circumstances specific to those students; however, when seven or eight students struggle to adhere to classroom rules and expectations, there is likely something instructional or procedurally that has missed the mark. Take this scenario:

> *A teacher struggles with the unruly behavior of several students in her 5th grade class. She shares with a colleague that the students are disorderly, disrespectful, and attention-seeking. Her colleague asks clarifying questions. What types of student behaviors is she experiencing? How does disrespect sound and look in her classroom? What policies and procedures are in place to ensure a positive classroom culture?*

The colleague was leading the teacher down a journey of examining classroom culture and climate as reasons for student misbehavior. While the teacher was looking outward at students' behaviors, the colleague was leading her inward to reflect on her practices and procedures. Great time and attention should be paid to adopting a definition of a positive classroom (and school) climate that is generated by and understood by all. Dedicating time to bring about a common set of norms and goals with an emphasis on safe and supportive relationships among class/school members is instrumental to academic and behavioral success. A common working definition (with examples) of healthy cultures enables both students and adults to recognize healthy and unhealthy climates when they experience them.

Teachers and leaders must be careful that schools don't become cliquish, exclusive clubs instead of vibrant, respectful, unified communities. Sadly, we are living in fairly uncivil times and disturbing and offensive behavior has been widely modeled to our kids. If this country is to move forward in a respectful, empathetic manner in service of unity, school systems will be at the center of that effort. How we teach perspective taking and civil discourse will dictate the types and depth of conversations that occur in our classrooms, among our colleagues, and in our families.

Ensuring every student knows they are valued members of the school community starts with the relationships built between adults and students, among adults, and among students. Every child has a right to a school environment that is respectful and appreciative of their unique skills, traditions, and heritage. Every one of us has experienced the agony of feeling excluded or devalued. At some point in our lives, we found ourselves on the outside looking in, feeling like we don't fit or belong. Sometimes this experience is a result of our interactions with family, colleagues, friends, or neighbors. While we cannot always control this type of experience for ourselves or others, we can commit to preventing our students from feeling this way in our classrooms, hallways, locker rooms, or rehearsal spaces. As champions for all students, we must ensure that we have infrastructures and systems in place that prevent students from falling off the radar and falling out of any meaningful connections at school. We are accountable for providing a school experience filled with meaningful relationships and consequential experiences, in and out of the classroom.

Let students hold you accountable to yourself and them. Survey your students about their experience with you in the classroom, on the stage, field, or court. Better yet, as a nod to candor, let someone else distribute and compile the survey data and comments. Whether you are a teacher, coach, or administrator, the outcome of these surveys should not feel like someone is out to get you; rather, that someone is out to help you grow as a professional and provide the optimal learning environment for all your students. Embrace this as an opportunity for self-reflection leading to clarity for the culture you wish to promote and the core values you expect of yourself and others.

EYES ON CULTURE IN ACTION

Clearly define expectations: Setting the tone for the learning environment requires a direct communication of expectations, procedures, and policies. This will look very different in an elementary classroom than a secondary classroom. There can be rules established by the teacher or determined by students. Finding a blend between the two will better serve all students. Shifting the conversation from *rules* to *agreements* also promotes student ownership and accountability. They own those principles they *agreed* to as part of the classroom decisions. Asking students to write briefly about each of the agreements (keep it simple, 4-6 agreements) and why they think the rules/agreements are important or how they will support them to be successful in class is an excellent tool for integration and self-reflection. This same process can be conducted by coaches, directors, and club leaders to support an "I got you" culture instead of a "Gotcha" culture.

Focus on respect: Respectful schools value the voices of all members as a top priority. Taking time to create procedures and including students in shaping the expectations for student engagement will generate discussions around what respect sounds and feels like to individual members. Expecting mutual respect in the school environment is essential to alleviating academic and behavioral challenges. Asking students what they would or would not change about their school or how the staff can support students more effectively elevates student voice and experience. Surveying students provides a more global picture of the experience students and staff are having in school.

Let students get to know you: Share a bit of yourself with your students so they see you as a whole person—not just their teacher/administrator. Far too many students, at every grade level, see teachers or principals as those who get put in a closet at 3:30 p.m. and let out the next day at 7:30 a.m. You can tell how connected your students feel to you when they see you out in public. If they see you in the grocery store or a restaurant and appear shocked that you eat, they probably don't see you as a parent, partner, sibling, or a child yourself. Sharing a bit about yourself, without oversharing personal information, humanizes you, and creates space for connection with your students.

Create opportunities for students to get to know each other: Emphasizing mutually respectful student-to-student relationships can serve as the foundation for a positive classroom/school culture. This starts by first knowing the names of your students *and* pronouncing them correctly. Close enough doesn't cut it. Pronouncing student names correctly is a sign of respect. It's equally important to know more than just their names—what are their interests, passions, strengths, and challenges? When people know others better, they treat them better. This takes time, but focusing on building classroom community by committing the time and activities to get to know one another will pay dividends. This can involve a simple activity such as "Would you rather…?" or a more complex activity in which students share something about what they value and why. Humanizing one another is indispensable to building community.

Be likable: *Kids don't learn from people they don't like.* This is actually the title of a book (Aspy & Roebuck, 1983). This sentiment made a comeback in Rita Pierson's 2013 TedTalk. It's a harsh reality, but it is the truth. Teachers who enter a classroom crabby, critical, or closed will struggle to form relationships with their students and colleagues. Teachers and school leaders need to be relational. Administrators who focus on rules and regulations without genuine, personal concern for the students and staff they are serving will be viewed strictly as authority figures who do nothing to promote students' voices, staff input, or mutual respect.

Be accessible with a servant spirit: Teachers and school leaders are more accessible today than ever—phone, text, Google voice, email, social media, etc. We can be accessible through the available communication tools and be inaccessible for emotional support and care at the same time. Simply being accessible does not ensure that your availability is fruitful. The spirit of your accessibility makes the difference and our openness will signal how accessible we truly want to be. Have you ever had a student come to you after school needing a classroom unlocked? The accessible adult will respond and perhaps begrudgingly unlock the room. The accessible adult with a servant spirit is available and joyfully unlocks the door and engages the student in conversation. The student leaves feeling as though they were the reason for your work and not an interruption of it. Some adults have an uncanny ability to make students feel as though they are a disruption instead of a pleasant diversion.

Responding to Disruptive Behavior

Disruptive behavior can derail a lesson, practice, or rehearsal. Left unchecked, disruptive behavior can quickly become the norm. It is important to recognize that misbehavior is more than just an interruption to the teaching taking place. It is also a form of communication. Getting to the cause of misbehavior is essential in correcting it. Misbehavior is often a result of frustration or stress which may or may not be related to the school environment. When students are frustrated or stressed about their learning experiences, they can act out. In some cases, students would rather be perceived as defiant than the internal message referring to themselves as "dumb." To prevent disruptions to student experiences, we must first determine what constitutes a disruption.

Simply put, disruption is a behavior that interferes with the ability of the teacher (coach, director) to teach and the student's (athlete, performer) ability to learn. Disruptive behavior can be as simple as talking while others are talking or asking off-topic questions. Disruptive behaviors can also be as complex as a student lashing out at peers and adults to the point that the student needs to be removed from the learning environment. Students may become disruptive because of personal circumstances including anxiety, depression, learning differences, or simply being hungry. Students can also become disorderly because the process and procedures in the learning environment are inconsistent or unclear. Discovering the motivation behind student behavior assists in redirecting inappropriate behavior to more positive, respectful conduct. Student (mis)behavior has been studied for years, most notably by Rudolf Dreikurs and Loren Grey (1993), whose premise is that all behavior—positive or negative—Is designed to achieve social recognition. Student misbehavior was classified into four categories (Braun, 2019):

1. *Gaining attention*: Students behave in ways that provide them attention, even if it is negative. Students can seek attention by tattling on others, constantly raising their hand in class, being the "class clown," or bullying and harassing others.

2. *Attempt to gain power; control*: When students cannot gain attention through their disruptive behavior, they resort to trying to control others. This behavior can range from arguing, crying, or lying, to throwing temper tantrums and openly defying adults.

3. *Exacting revenge or retaliation*: Because some students cannot assume responsibility for their actions, students will lash out at others for their behavior, especially when they perceive they have been treated unjustly. They may trip others, knock books to the ground, verbally abuse others and break equipment. This behavior can escalate further, even to the point of being threatening and dangerous.

4. *Displaying inadequacies*: Students who lack skills or academic abilities may hide that reality by not participating in learning activities or simply giving up. They would rather be perceived as disruptive than "dumb."

Regardless of the motivation behind the student behavior, the disruption has occurred and has interrupted the learning process. Responding to student misbehavior is complex but how adults respond has a direct impact on the disorderly student as well as everyone else in the classroom. While diffusing a situation, be cautious about power struggles. Any time adults flex their muscle of authority, the battle for power is on and no one will win. Yes, as adults, you can punish children. You can call them out in front of classmates. You can even raise your voice at them or use physical proximity to gain compliance. This approach does not change student behavior, it simply teaches children how you will weaponize your authority to maintain power.

You lose no power as a teacher or principal (or parent for that matter) by sharing power with students (children). Student tardiness serves as an example of power struggles. If a student is tardy to class, should there be a consequence? Absolutely. Does it need to be addressed only through punishment? No. Trying to understand why the student is tardy is far more important than punishing the behavior. Asking the student what is making it difficult for her to get to class on time can be an expression of concern. Resolving

> When we operate from absolutes, the opportunity to strengthen the relationship with students is overlooked.

the tardiness problem can be mutually agreed upon. Does the student have to serve the detention that day? Can we build a better connection by asking the student which day would work best for her? Before or after school? When we operate from absolutes, the opportunity to strengthen the relationship with students is overlooked.

EYES ON CULTURE IN ACTION

Respond immediately, clearly, and directly: Managing disruptive behavior is a balancing act between not overreacting or underreacting. Most important is to react and respond—ignoring disruptive behavior is a sure-fire way for such behavior to continue and escalate. Explain to the student how their behavior is disrupting the learning environment. Provide opportunities for students to course correct.

Address the behavior as privately as possible: Be careful not to call out negative student behavior in front of classmates (unless of course, the behavior is dangerous to the student or others). In a private conversation, asking the student clarifying questions can help the student understand how their behavior is impacting others and may help the staff member better understand the motives behind the presenting behavior:

+ Is something interfering with your ability to participate productively in class? Is anyone bothering you? Something upsetting to you? Are you sleeping OK? Are you hungry?
+ Is there something I am doing that is upsetting you? Someone else?
+ Do you need a break from this for a couple of minutes? Get a drink of water? Take a quick walk in the hallway?

Respond to disrespectful behavior with greater respect: Remember, behavior is a form of communication. When students lash out, swear, throw items, etc., it is their way of telling you that things are out of order for them. The louder the student gets, the quieter and softer the adult needs to be. The more disrespectful the student gets, the greater respect the adult must extend.

Get curious, not furious: Rebecca Alber studies stress and trauma-related behaviors. She advocates for teachers to get curious about why students act out and realize that classroom outbursts, defiance, and volatility can be symptomatic of repeated exposure to neglect, abuse, and violence. This approach allows adults to respond to student behaviors rather than react to them (Alber, 2016).

Recognize the difference between punishment and consequence: For this purpose, punishment is defined as "the way we use our authority to gain compliance." Punishment issued by a parent, principal, or coach is designed to use authority as a means to deter the same behavior in the future. Consequence, on the other hand, is the way we use our authority to help students develop self-discipline so the next time they can accept responsibility for and modify their behavior. A student can be given a consequence without being punished.

Provide reassurance: When a student's emotions are raw—crying, throwing things, yelling, kicking—they need assurance from adults. They need to be told, "You are OK. We will work through this." Students need to know that their misbehavior is simply their way of telling us that something isn't right. They need to know that their behavior, at that moment, does not reflect their character or their heart and that we are going to help them get through. They need us to speak to them the way we would want an adult to speak to our own child.

Discipline: An Opportunity For Teaching And Learning

A positive school culture requires healthy, supportive personal relationships and clear expectations for academic and personal behaviors. The benefits of a climate of this caliber include increased time and attention to the instruction and decreased negative student behaviors. The foundation of successful behavior management rests in relationships. Effective discipline does not focus merely on punishment. Discipline comes from the Latin word *"disciplinare,"* which means, *"to teach."*

Developing common language around expectations for student behavior increases the chances of students understanding what is expected of them and why. Schmoker states that "clarity precedes competence" (2004, p. 85). Teachers and leaders must provide clear expectations and the subsequent outcomes when they are not met. To take this a step further, *how* we communicate those expectations matters as much as the expectations themselves.

It is easy to identify what a school values in terms of discipline from the second a visitor steps foot into the school. Are there lots of rules posted everywhere? That, in and of itself, is not a problem, depending on the language used to convey rules. Take two schools with the same rules and expectations around food in the classrooms, for example. The sign for *School A* reads: "To maintain a positive learning environment for you and your classmates, please dispose of food before entering classrooms. Thank you!" The sign for *School B* reads: "ABSOLUTELY NO FOOD ALLOWED!!!" It is the same rule for both schools, but the delivery is significantly different and likely received differently by students, parents, and guests to the school. Positive adult-student relationships start with respect as the foundation. Framing messages in a respectful tone will more likely result in understanding and compliance.

How we discipline students is directly related to the culture and climate of a school. Discipline that is fair, patient, progressive, compassionate, and loving leads to trust among students and adults and pride in the school. Discipline that is random, unpredictable, intolerant, and punitive results in anger, mistrust, and withdrawal. Schools that value a positive school climate take the time to make sure students not only know what the rules are, but also understand the logic behind the rules because it has been explained to them.

Does your school merely identify the rules and expectations or are the reasons for the rules and expectations also explained? For example, many schools do not allow hats in the building. Most schools simply state that as a rule and issue consequences to any offenders. Is it possible students don't follow certain rules because they don't understand them? Adults can ask students to remove their hats. Compliant students will remove them and may even leave them off; however, many will remove the hat when asked only to place it back on their head once they are out of view of the staff member. Focus on educating, not punishing. Leaders don't just tell others what to do—they inspire others to discover new things on their own, initiate their own ideas, and solve their own problems. Imagine the response if a staff member asked a student to remove their hat and followed that request up with the following:

> *"Do you know why we don't permit hats in the building? We have a responsibility to make sure the people in our building belong here. When people are wearing hats we can't see faces clearly, making it difficult to determine if they belong on campus. From a safety standpoint, we need to be able to see everyone's faces." Once the logic behind the rule has been explained, it's important to keep the communication lines open. "Think about what I have shared with you and if you still have questions or concerns about the hat rule, please come back and talk with me about it."*

Closing the conversation this way does three things:

1. It tells the student there is a specific reason for the rule's existence.
2. It signals that student and staff safety is important.
3. It keeps the door open for further conversation and a path for students to provide alternative suggestions.

It is imperative to clearly communicate the school's behavior standards and consequences with students and parents/guardians. While a school handbook can't possibly cover every conceivable behavior scenario, the handbook should reflect the standards for behavior so students know what is expected of them. See this sample message for parents/guardians and students:

> *The goal is for all students to develop and learn social, emotional, and behavioral competence supporting their academic engagement. Educators strive to develop positive, predictable, and safe environments that promote strong interpersonal relationships with students through teaching, modeling, and encouragement. To that end, students will be expected to adhere to school policies and conduct themselves in a respectful manner with their peers and staff to foster a safe, orderly school that is focused on learning and positive relationships.*

Equally important is outlining for students their rights when it comes to the school environment. For example, students have the right to:

+ A safe and orderly learning environment.
+ Courteous and respectful treatment by staff and other students.
+ A quality education with clear, challenging learning goals designed to prepare students for their future.
+ A supportive learning environment and appropriate progressive correction when conduct does not meet expectations.

- Access to curriculum, school/district services, and extracurricular activities.
- Access to social, emotional, and behavioral health resources.
- Know and annually review the district behavior expectations and potential consequences when violated.
- Equal treatment in the enforcement of school rules and procedures.

Students and parents/guardians should be well informed under what circumstances students will be held accountable and disciplined for misconduct such as:

- When students engage in conduct that disrupts the orderly and efficient operation of the school or school activity.
- When conduct disrupts the rights of other students to obtain their education or to participate in school activities.
- When conduct interrupts an optimal learning environment for all students and staff.

Even the most effective communication about school rules, policies, and procedures and the rationale for their existence is not going to prevent all discipline issues from occurring. Students are going to have missteps. They are going to make poor choices and use bad judgment. They are going to disrupt, interrupt, and interfere with the learning process, even when that is not their intent. We cannot assume that misbehavior reflects the personal character of that student.

EYES ON CULTURE IN ACTION

Lead with kindness: Even those with the most egregious misbehaviors deserve our kindness. Students (and adults) act out for a variety of reasons, but it often comes from a previous experience of mistreatment they endured from someone else. When others are most broken and most wounded, they need our kindness as a model to get better, be better, and behave better.

Practice patience: Sometimes teachers, leaders, and parents think they need to respond immediately to the information about discipline matters. In our haste, we risk making knee-jerk decisions, missing some key information, and disciplining others based on emotion rather than expectations. Don't feel like you have to give a response or issue a consequence right away. Instead of issuing the length of a suspension immediately following a fight, for example, inform students and parents that the student will go home while the matter is being reviewed. This gives you time to review situations, compare them to other comparable events for consistency and equity purposes, and consider the logic behind your decisions. Following up with parents/guardians regarding disciplinary decisions is imperative. While extending patience to the one who has violated school rules is important, so too is granting patience with the process. Sometimes we need to slow down to hurry up.

Monitor volume and tone: How easy is it to become elevated and agitated with a student (or staff member) over a discipline matter? When you come upon a situation, do you respond to the hollering student who is unable to manage her emotions by yelling at her more loudly? When students are handling themselves in that manner, they have lost their ability to regulate their emotions and reactions. They have lost their ability to be reasonable or rational. When adults start yelling, the situation can often escalate further. In those instances, the adult needs to raise their compassion, not their voice. The louder a student yells, the softer our voice needs to get. The more out of control they become, the gentler our tone needs to be. The more disrespectful they are, the greater respect we need to extend. When we respond disrespectfully, louder, and more harshly, we are not extending excellence to students. We are not teaching them and we definitely will not reach them. We can and need to model to them through our tone, volume, and body language that we are with them. We will support them and we love them even when they behave in really unlovable ways.

Focus on the relationships that have been damaged instead of the rules that have been broken: When a student is disrespectful to a classmate or adult, the rules around respect are not the only things broken. The relationship between the student and the injured party is damaged and in need of repair. When a student steals something from a classmate, a rule is broken and a sense of safety is violated, but the trust between the two is also fractured. Yes, a school "rule" has been broken, but by strictly focusing on the disrespectful words or behaviors hurled by the student, we lose the opportunity to repair the relationship that was damaged.

Lead with discipline, not punishment: Anyone in a position of authority knows they have power. Punishment is about power; discipline is about teaching self-control leading to self-discipline. Approach discipline with the intent to improve the problem-solving and self-management skills of the rule violator.

Avoid arguing: Students do not have to be right *and* have the last word; neither do you. It's the most unproductive combination imaginable in any relationship. Know when to pull back and let the student have the last word—at least at that moment.

Don't punish groups out of anger and frustration. Sometimes students and even colleagues can get on our very last nerve. We may find ourselves reminding students repeatedly to start or stop doing something that violates classroom agreements. Out of frustration, we forget to teach and start to punish. Examples of this include canceling recess, silent lunches, or class detentions. Teachers (rightly so) do not appreciate administrators issuing global messages about staff behavior. They don't want a universal address; they want the administration to instead deal with the individual teachers. The same is true for students. Deal with the offenders, not the entire group.

Assure your care and concern for the student: Acknowledge the emotion presented by the student: "I hear you and how upset you are. We will work through this together."

Maynard and Weinstein (2019) talk about using the "iceberg perspective" when looking at behavior, meaning there are almost always other issues packed under the behavior. School officials need to understand the function of the presenting behavior. In some cases, the function of the behaviors can be rooted in emotional or physical needs. When students are frustrated, anxious, or feeling marginalized, the raw emotions around these feelings can result in unacceptable behavior. Additionally, when tired, hungry, or dehydrated, students can easily become irritated and act out. At this point, it's critically important to let the child be heard—even if it's defensive and argumentative. In contrast to punishing, teachers and school leaders can use discipline as a means to teach, provide guidance, and influence.

> In contrast to punishing, teachers and school leaders can use discipline as a means to teach, provide guidance, and influence.

The Internal Siren

A high school teacher was asked by the school registrar to give Annie an incomplete grade for the quarter. The registrar explained that the principal was aware of the student's absences and would follow up with the teacher. The teacher was furious that Annie would be allowed an incomplete for a grade when she hadn't done the assigned homework, didn't make up the tests or quizzes she missed, and consistently slept through class. When the principal followed up with the teacher, she explained that she was frustrated and resentful that he was allowing Annie to receive an incomplete. Annie never came to the teacher to make up her work, she slept during class, and hadn't even taken some of the tests. The principal listened empathetically to the teacher, then proceeded to let her know that Annie's family had been evicted and homeless for the better part of the school quarter and this is why he was permitting the incomplete. Immediately, the teacher's tone changed to one of understanding, empathy, and a willingness to help the student in any way. The teacher said, "I didn't know that's what was going on with her." The principal responded, "I've learned over time when I have felt the same as you are feeling now that we don't need to know the details of a student's story to extend compassion and grace to them." The principal pressed further, "Was any internal siren going off in you that something might be interfering with her ability to succeed in your class?"

This likely was not an easy conversation for the principal to have with the teacher but it was a necessary coaching conversation. This type of scenario takes place every day in schools, work environments, and homes. We tend to be rigid in our thoughts and attitudes because we often view situations from only one perspective. If we are truly champions for all students, we must commit to working through issues of this nature. We must be willing to engage in open, honest, and constructive conversations. This requires us to candidly identify topics that are high-tension topics, acknowledge differences of opinions, and get real about our intentions in our dialogues.

It might help to think of these situations as more of a coaching process than having difficult conversations. When you develop trusting relationships with staff and students, it becomes easier to provide feedback that might be difficult to hear. We all have an internal siren that tells us something isn't right, someone is out of order, or something needs to be addressed—feeling like a colleague isn't doing their part, teachers not communicating adequately with students or parents, or grading practices that focus more on executive functioning and less on student learning, for example. We tend to avoid difficult conversations because we fear the potential outcome or consequences. Listening to your internal siren, though, can be an act of courage. People often view courage as some monumental effort—professionally blowing the whistle on someone else, a firefighter going into a burning building, or refusing to give up a seat during the Civil Rights movement. While these certainly are acts of courage, we can act courageously in simple, ordinary ways. Acts of courage may include:

+ Asking someone out on a date.
+ Saying "I love you" first.
+ Standing up for another person being mistreated.
+ Saying "I am sorry."
+ Initiating a difficult conversation.

A friend had a major falling out with other family members more than twenty-five years ago. Whatever the details surrounding the reasons for the fallout, the outcome has not changed. The family members do not speak to one another. Recently, the friend had a major health crisis and the news of that got back to her parents. While dealing with this crisis, she came home to a voice message on the home answering machine. It was from her father, whom she had not spoken to in twenty-five years. Her father wanted her to know that he was thinking of her and praying for his daughter. He ended the message by saying he hoped they could talk sometime. Placing that phone call was an incredible act of courage. The father listened to the internal siren signaling to him that he needed to respond to the news by reaching out to his daughter. As mentioned previously, difficult conversations need to take place in most aspects of our lives.

EYES ON CULTURE IN ACTION

Initiate a conversation you've been avoiding: Being honest and direct with others prevents minor issues from ballooning into major ones. It prevents benign issues from metastasizing and spreading. When leaders engage in uncomfortable conversations, staff members become willing to do that among themselves. This results in respectful and productive outcomes. Are you feeling like a colleague isn't doing their fair share as part of your team?

Be direct without being offensive: How you say something is as important as what is said. Focus on the strengths and character of the other person when bringing up issues of concern. For example, if an administrator says something insensitive to an employee or student, good feedback would be to point out that the administrator has too much of a history of being supportive and concerned for others and that the insensitive comment doesn't reflect their heart or character. Message delivered, personal integrity intact.

Interrupt the pattern: In our effort to dodge difficult conversations, is our avoidance condoning and even accommodating bad behavior from someone else? Interrupting the pattern of avoidance is a way to champion for others and it need not be limited to our students or colleagues. Do you need to have a conversation with your mother about her treatment of your spouse? Do you need to talk to that sibling who still owes you the money you loaned him? These types of situations take place in everyday life but can quickly become contentious. We can champion for others through our willingness to identify situations that serve as a source of tension and address them in a direct, clear, and productive way.

What Do You Need Me to Better Understand?

To be a champion for students requires a level of maturity on the part of adults. The kind of maturity that knows when to lean in and when to back off. When to ask more questions and when to listen or be willing to just sit in silence. When dealing with student discipline issues, we need to assess the scope of the circumstance and attempt to understand the experiences and feelings students bring to the situation. It's important to remember that behavior is another form of communication and it often tells at least part of the story of another person. When we try to better understand the reasons behind the behavior, we are more equipped to provide guidance, influence thinking and emotions, and help frame the situation so others can discover a path forward.

Take this example from a junior high teacher who provided every opportunity and every support to a student to help him be successful. The young man continued to reject the assistance the teacher was providing and refused to engage in class activities and assignments. Day after day he would come to class and put his head down and sleep and day after day the teacher would prod and poke him to participate, review information with him, and make herself available to him before or after school. On one particularly frustrating day, the teacher lashed out at him at the end of the class and said, "If you are not going to do anything, you don't even need to come back to class tomorrow." The incident had been reported to the principal by another student who felt uncomfortable by the teacher's proclamation. The teacher recounted the incident this way:

"I already knew I shouldn't have said what I did. I was just so frustrated. My principal asked me what bothered me most about the situation. I told him, "I am so offended that he will not participate at all. I work my ass off to plan lessons, grade papers, and provide support. He doesn't even have the decency to keep his head up or respond when called on." The principal looked right at me and said, "Why does this offend you? Why do you feel his behavior is even about you?" I couldn't explain why I felt the way I did. My principal let me sit with my feelings and didn't make me feel like I had to change my feelings to appease him. After sitting in silence for a while, he said to me, "What do you need me to better understand?" It was probably the most important thing he could have said to me because I didn't feel judged and I felt his sincerity in wanting to know how he could help me.

Everyone is faced with situations that can pull us emotionally in a variety of directions, testing our very ability to manage our own emotions. Telling the student to not even bother coming back to class was the teacher's impulsive response. Even the best teachers can lose their cool. In this scenario, the principal used this as a teachable moment for the teacher. Great leaders are great teachers at heart. They help others discover for themselves what they want to do rather than merely gaining compliance with what the leader wants them to do. Teachers want to know they matter. They want to know if what they feel and have to say about their experience matters. The same is true for students. They want to know if they matter—whether they behave well or not. Many students with challenging behaviors have experienced a great deal of emotional turbulence—living in environments of disarray, confusion, and even violence. When they come to us, they have not always had models of self-awareness and self-management in their lives.

EYES ON CULTURE IN ACTION

Don't be offended: When we are offended by the words, tone, or behavior of others, a nerve has likely been hit. The second agreement in *The Four Agreements* (1997) is: Don't take anything personally. The situation with the junior high teacher illuminates how personally offended she was by the student's indifference to her class. In reality, the student's behavior had nothing to do with the teacher. While everyone has experiences of feeling slighted, those who are offended easily are robbed of peace and joy.

Navigate with maturity: Addressing inappropriate student behavior and emotions requires adults to proceed calmly, with compassion and maturity. L.R. Knost's quote applies beautifully in this situation: "When little people are overwhelmed by emotions, it's our job to share our calm, not join their chaos." (2019) The same applies to big people!

Avoid responding with anger: Addressing student hostility and aggression with adult hostility and aggression will exacerbate the situation. Adults need to be the voice of reason, compassion, and calm when students are out of order. Remember, the louder students get, the quieter we need to respond. The more disrespectful they are, the greater respect we need to extend.

Avoid becoming defensive: Responses such as, "Don't you dare speak to me like that" will likely be more triggering than productive. Breathe—calm people are breathers and bringing calmness to contentious situations is a gift.

The Power Has Always Been Within You

A school counselor recounted an interaction with Emily, a junior student, and her family. Just before the start of a school year, the counselor met with Emily's family, who wanted to be proactive in getting a plan to help their daughter be more successful that school year than she had been previously. The counselor applauded the family's effort to get ahead of potential problems. When they met, the counselor asked Emily if she had any insights as to why she struggled the previous school year. Emily was able to identify two things:

1. *She is stubborn*: Emily said she doesn't like to ask for help and isn't comfortable admitting she needs help. The counselor asked her how her stubbornness was working for her. She smiled her beautiful smile and said, "Not very well."
2. *She is the problem in her family*: Her words, not her parents. She said she doesn't take care of her schoolwork, can be disrespectful, and is moody.

As they talked further, it became apparent that Emily's lack of academic success, combined with her seemingly nonchalant attitude about it, had taken a toll on her entire family. Mom shared how stressed she was feeling all the time, dad was walking a tightrope trying to support both mom and Emily, and it was clear the entire family was held hostage by whether the daughter kept up with her coursework. The counselor later relayed that she thought that conversation with Emily and her family could have taken place with any number of families in the community. As champions for children, what can be learned from this situation?

Children who behave disrespectfully do so because they have been allowed to—not because they want to: Respect starts at home, but must be reinforced at school. Helping parents see the value of demanding respect among family members is crucial. Parents need to make the commitment to expect their children to reserve their best manners for each other—not the neighbor kids, not their classmates, and not their teammates. Children should be expected to use their best manners with their siblings. Children who regularly exercise good manners at home *generally* exhibit good manners everywhere else. If children are not used to that expectation, schools need to cultivate it and foster positive relationships among students through the expectation of good manners with one another. Good manners contribute to increased self-confidence and self-respect.

Children must learn to advocate for themselves. Emily's mother had twisted herself inside out trying to develop every strategy to get Emily to do her homework and pass her classes. The counselor advised the mom to let Emily develop some skills herself. Emily and her counselor developed a plan for what the student would do when she didn't understand instructions, got stuck on homework, or fell behind. It required Emily to ask for help and seek the assistance of others. As parents (and educators), we must assist our children in developing the skills necessary to ask for help, advocate for themselves, and problem solve.

We must guard against handicapping our children (students) by attempting to make life too easy for them. Parents with new infants have been told by their pediatrician to let babies cry for a while so they can learn how to comfort themselves. In a similar spirit, we must let developing children learn how to help themselves. Parents cannot be all things to their children at all times and teachers can't be all things to all students either. Although it can be difficult to watch kids struggle, a lot can be learned from adversity. It's not fun, it's not glamorous, but it is necessary to struggle to develop problem-solving skills and resilience.

Teach kids how to click their heels. When parents are scared, they grip tighter. Emily was able to identify all that she lost by not performing well in school—loss of academic credit, disqualification from competing in athletics, cell phone, family privileges, and she was required to attend summer school. The greater the parental fear, the tighter the grip. In the final scene of *The Wizard of Oz* Dorothy can go home by clicking her ruby red slippers. Bewildered, Dorothy asked, "That's all I needed to do?" Glenda, the good witch, told Dorothy the *power was always within her*. We must help our children recognize the personal power they have over their lives and their futures.

Managing Adult Missteps

You can take any current event—political, social, or cultural—and relate it to the role of a teacher or leader. What can we learn about the teacher arrested for an inappropriate relationship with a student? Or the administrator who is under the influence of alcohol at school? And when a teacher falsifies a student record, what is our takeaway? When a student physically assaults another student with a bystander recording the event? Or the athletic team that engages in a hazing tradition resulting in serious injury or death of a student? Any time these events hit the news ask yourself the following questions: What would I do in this situation? How would I handle that? While we can learn much about our leadership style and core values through the successes of others, sometimes we can learn as much (or more) from their failures. Although these types of situations are not the norm and include a small percentage of the profession, they generate the most publicity and often the information is inaccurate. The reality, though, is that for all the time and energy we put into helping children identify their missteps and learn from their mistakes, do we afford the same to the adults who have fallen short of professional and ethical standards?

Take this scenario:

> At the end of a school day, a teacher comes to your office and asks an innocuous question about an upcoming school event. In the course of your discussion, you notice the teacher's speech is slurred. Though you initially worry about a health issue like a stroke, you

*quickly notice the teacher seems impaired in other ways—an inability to maintain balance, eyes darting and seemingly bloodshot, and incoherent thinking. It dawns on you very quickly that the teacher is possibly drunk. As you inquire, the teacher admits to drinking alcohol while on campus **and** while performing professional duties. What are your next steps?*

Know your district and your building-level rules and due process procedures. You need to ascertain if the matter is a violation of school policy or if there is a violation of the law. If it is the latter, notify local police immediately. If the violation involves a student or colleague, make sure you report it to your supervisor immediately. If someone you supervise is out of order, report it to the central office or your human resource director, if you have one. Many districts do not, so it is incumbent upon you to read and review the policies and respond accordingly. Before moving on to any situation involving a student or staff member who may be out of order, review your policies.

Talk it out. Remember, you don't have to go it alone when faced with a colleague or someone you supervise who violates a policy. Every difficult situation you will encounter will have a solution, but you don't always have to be the one to come up with it. Very few situations involving the behavior of others are crystal clear—there is usually a certain amount of ambiguity. Talking the situation over with someone who can provide input and insights helps to clarify your process as you move forward. By surrounding yourself with thoughtful, critical thinkers, you will be better equipped to process the situation at hand. When confronting challenging situations, are we surrounded by skilled, analytical thinkers and problem solvers? Are we surrounded by competent people who reflect on policies and procedures? School leaders must view divergent opinions and perspectives as invaluable when dealing with situations that may result in disciplinary measures for students or staff. Proactively communicating code of conduct expectations and consequences for failing to meet them diminishes ambiguity and inconsistent application of consequences. Mismanagement of this important administrative role can result in the kind of division that negatively impacts the school community.

EYES ON CULTURE IN ACTION

Uncover facts and eliminate ambiguity: School leaders must be thorough, fair, and objective in handling student discipline and employee code of conduct situations. We must ask questions, followed by more questions. We must also acquire as much factual and objective information as possible. We must ask ourselves, "Do I have enough information to make decisions? Am I making decisions too quickly without the information or conducting the necessary interviews?" Leadership isn't easy—asking tough questions and holding people accountable isn't easy either. Another question worth posing: "If this situation were to hit the front page of our newspaper, would it result in widespread (not universal) praise or criticism?" Getting it right takes time, patience, and thorough fact-finding.

Be fair and consistent in the application of policies: Nothing sends a school culture into flames faster than inconsistency and the appearance of favoritism. Ultimately, as school leaders, we must live on the corner of *fairness* and *consistency*. In addition to reviewing district policies, review outcomes of other, similar situations. What was the justification behind the outcomes of those decisions? What applies to the current situation you are dealing with?

Be peaceful: School leaders need to make peace with the fact that other people will (falsely) talk about situations and you won't be able to respond. Being on the receiving end of such false accusations about the way a situation was handled is never fun, but keep it in perspective. Is the criticism leveled by those who have accurate information? Are people publicly commenting on a matter in your school to help the school get better or just to take shots at leadership? The advent of social media has made school leaders public targets with people making wild, false claims. Effective leaders are not going to make everyone happy and if they do, there are likely issues that are being avoided and going unaddressed.

Focus on the best interests of students: Always, *always* act in the best interest of students when it comes to missteps. At the heart of every discipline issue, a child is affected in some way. Either as the subject of the misbehavior of adults or peers or the ones who are out of order themselves. Discipline matters are teaching and learning opportunities but the safety, security, and dignity of students must always come first.

Share information when and where you can: In the absence of direct information, people make up their narrative which is often erroneous. To the extent that it is possible to objectively share what you can, do so with those who need to know.

Discipline with dignity: You can discipline others and love and care about them at the same time. As intentional as we have to be in helping students move forward when they don't meet standards for acceptable behavior, it is equally important to help adults when they have lapses in judgment. Always remember the most effective and professional teacher, coach, para, or principal can lose it all with an act of bad judgment—taking money, saying inappropriate things to students, allowing the mistreatment of a student, retaliating against someone, or arriving to work under the influence. Effective, professional, and caring adults have been disciplined and/or lost their jobs because of poor judgment, not because they are bad people; when that happens, they need to know that you still care about them.

CHAPTER 3

Core Principle 2:
Expect Excellence - Culturizing Student Activities

The essence of a positive school experience rests in the school culture. A positive school culture begins with leadership and thrives on the positive mindsets of all adults in the school. A school culture uniquely forms and fosters the mindsets of students in the school. Positive school culture is composed of lots of nuances—the welcoming manner from the school's main office personnel, the tone of the school's communications, the quality of facilities, cleanliness of the school, and the way students are featured and highlighted throughout the building. When visitors enter a school building, it takes only minutes to determine if it is an environment in which they want to be a part. This is true for potential teachers, coaches, directors, support staff, students, and their families.

While administrators must ensure they are putting the best teachers in all classrooms, they must also put the best people in coaching, directing, and club sponsor positions. If you ask adults what their best school experience was, answers often include their experience in an extracurricular activity—sports, music, drama, speech and debate, service groups, intramurals, clubs, and activities. Student-centered programs encourage student participation and serve as a source of joy and pride for students for years to come. Students will give blood, sweat, and tears when they believe the adults overseeing their program genuinely care about them and operate in the best interests of the team, cast, club, or group.

EYES ON CULTURE IN ACTION

Programs are student-centered: Students who feel valued and included are committed, challenged, and joyful. Student-centered programs result in students feeling valued and a part of something bigger than themselves. Do the choir students seem alive when they are singing? Are the athletes being challenged to maximize their potential? Is there joy when students participate in the Spanish Club and Ping Pong Club? You can only look for these signs of student-centered programs by actually attending and monitoring them. Show up in the weight room, go to the play rehearsal, and let the jazz band entertain you. Assessing the quality of student programs requires an investment of time, resources, and exceptional adults who want to make a *positive* difference.

Students develop skills: Student-centered programs have a positive culture *and* students have an opportunity to grow and develop individual skills as well as collective ones. When students submit their writing to the classroom teacher, it is teacher feedback that assists them in improving as writers. Students involved in school programs also need feedback. The goal within student programs should be to level up the participants in simple but meaningful ways—strengthening an athletic or fine arts skill, developing communication and leadership proficiencies, and cultivating intrinsic motivation to improve. These improvements come with every interaction and providing feedback as often as possible (through text, email, or after lessons) reintroduces challenges and promotes student learning.

Students have ownership and power: Just like in the classroom, students are the ones who should be doing the work. As directors, coaches, advisors, and school leaders, we need to recognize that we lose no power as leaders by sharing power with students. Let them plan their theme nights for sporting events, design their T-shirts for the musical, write the editorial for the school newspaper about their club or organization. Share the social media accounts—give ownership to the students to promote the activities that mean the most to them. In this way, leaders can extend faith and confidence in their students and promote mutual trust.

Their ideas trump yours: The opportunities for athletes, musicians, student governments, and newspaper and yearbook staff do not necessarily meet the needs and interests of all students. Let students generate their ideas and plan events to involve more students—a ping pong club, gaming club, or an LGBTQ+ club. Yes, they will need guidance, but that is very different from needing direction. Let them, within the safe and supportive school environment, learn to lead.

Can a school culture do irreparable damage to a student or group of students? Absolutely. The State of Iowa is home to The University of Iowa and it is full of Hawkeyes through and through. You can imagine how painful it has been recently since the revelation of widespread mistreatment of Hawkeye football players. This was revealed in the wake of the death of George Floyd, the man who died at the knee of a Minneapolis police officer. The subsequent protests gave voice to student-athletes who felt the culture within the Iowa program was systemically racist, toxic, demeaning, and demoralizing. The first brave black players to speak about racial disparities in the program opened the door for other players to share their experience and their pain. With each revelation, shockwaves were sent across the State. From the outside, the Iowa football program was run by high-character people who helped get many players to the NFL or into the coaching profession. At the time, head coach Kirk Ferentz was in the midst of a 20+ year run and his strength and conditioning coach had been beside him throughout.

The stories the former players shared about the culture of the program, and specifically the weight room, illuminate what happens when adults are not held accountable for their behavior. "If you have an environment where the players don't feel like they can bring up an issue, that's a problem," Ferentz said. "I feel like I let those players down by not creating that environment where they did feel comfortable and sharing more about their experiences, bringing that to our attention, while they were here. Our coaches feel the same way, and we're committed to making sure that never happens again." (Rittenburg, 2020) After calling dozens of former players and asking for their feedback about their experience, Coach Ferentz acknowledged that those players provided him a new "awareness" and admitted he had "blind spots" in not recognizing problems that made black players feel mistreated or uncomfortable in his program. Another former player posted how he felt mistreated because of his ADHD. He indicated another member of the coaching staff called him "stupid" on more than one occasion and posted his grade point average on a team board. In addition to the systemic racism felt by black members of the squad, other members felt bullied and harassed by the coaching staff.

Ferentz stated publicly that he expected his staff to do better and he vowed to hold himself accountable to do better for all athletes in the program. The Iowa football program has since adopted a team advisory group, an opportunity for athletes to share with other teammates their concerns about the culture of the program, shore up communication with the coaching staff and challenge the climate in which they are expected to excel.

This type of behavior is not unique to the Iowa football program. As you read about this situation, are you thinking about pockets of disrespectful or demeaning behavior from a coach to athletes in your school? Do we explain this away as the coach is just trying to "toughen them up"? Does the play director ridicule the performers rather than coach them up? Are there pockets of parents, student-athletes, or fine arts students who are raising the red flag with you about the demeaning or retaliatory behavior of some adults in your building? Do you have a plan to address these issues?

When school leaders pause, listen, and dig deeper into the feedback about student experiences in school programs, we may learn there are bigger issues our students and parents are encountering (and even suffering). How do you ensure your students are not being mistreated, marginalized, or demeaned by adults on your staff?

EYES ON CULTURE IN ACTION

Define and promote school culture: How are school leaders summoned to address toxic culture issues such as retaliatory or intimidating behavior, for example? Whether the mistreatment is student-to-student, staff-to-student, or staff-to-staff, school leaders are responsible for setting high expectations and addressing toxic culture issues to move our schools forward so all students and staff can achieve at the highest levels in an optimal learning environment.

Tell adults what will and will not be tolerated: Clear is kind. Clarity of expectations with staff is critical. It would seem you should not have to tell adults in a school system how to treat those in their care, but they need to hear from you as a school leader what you expect. Is it acceptable to kick a student-athlete out of the weight room because a coach is frustrated with them? Are you comfortable with a director kicking a performer off the stage because they are not performing at the level the director expects? What about swearing at kids? Allowing the mocking of a student by others? If we are not directly telling adults what we expect in terms of culture, we are leaving it to chance. And, chances are, students will be mistreated in ways you may never know about.

Talk directly to the participants: As a leader of their school, tell students directly what type of experience you want them to have as part of your extracurricular programs. Tell them you want and need to know if they are not having a positive and respectful experience. Students and families need to know there is a lifeline beyond the coach or director. Telling students that you cannot help what you do not know instills a sense of ownership for their experiences. Make yourself available for their feedback either through face-to-face (the most effective) conversations, email, text, a suggestion box, direct message on school accounts, or an anonymous electronic tool that anyone can use to register concerns and compliments.

Expect respect: Teaching and expecting classmates, teammates, and castmates to treat one another with respect is essential to excellent school cultures. In this classroom, on this team, in these rehearsals...we will be respectful. In our words and our actions, we will be respectful. We must teach the behaviors we expect. Imagine if coaches or directors started their practices and rehearsals with lessons on respect—what it will look like and sound like, and what it won't. You can be assured that many of the issues staff and administration deal with center around student-to-student treatment. By teaching the expectation, you raise the character of students and reduce the negative experience students can have.

Take action: When a teacher gets a reputation for not updating their grade book or not providing adequate instruction, most administrators are all over that. We meet with the teacher immediately, review expectations, offer support and assistance, and follow-up to make sure the concerning behavior is corrected. What do we do when we hear that a coach or director is disrespectful or demeaning? As leaders and colleagues, we must be willing to raise the level of awareness and accountability when someone is out of order. We must be willing to say, "I'm not very comfortable with the way you are speaking to our team." This candor is not relegated solely to administrators. As educators, we must all be willing to step in when necessary.

Teaching Beyond The Classroom

Extracurricular activities can certainly be a source of pride and joy for the school and throughout the local community. Offering an assortment of programs to meet the talents and interests of all students is essential. These student activities should be an extension of the classroom in the variety of opportunities offered, the positive coaching provided, and the positive culture expected.

How often have we heard or said to others, "Life is short"? We try to impress upon ourselves, our children, and our students that time flies and we should make the most of the time we have, even if we don't know when one's life will come to an end. If you have ever had someone in your life with a terminal illness, "Life is short" becomes a battle cry. From the life-defining point of diagnosis, things that previously occupied their time, finances, and emotional energy get re-prioritized in record time. Recognizing that the quantity of their remaining days is narrowing, they turn their focus to the quality of those days. Conversely, there are a finite number of days in an athletic season, a play production, a school year. Regardless of the ups and downs of an activity, the blessings and challenges of a play production, or the highs and lows of an athletic season, there will be an end. How can we ensure the time is joyful rather than time spent with participants counting down the remaining days?

EYES ON CULTURE IN ACTION

Know your why: Do you have a clear purpose for teaching, coaching, directing? We usually find our why through reflection and experiences. Students profoundly impacted by a teacher may join the profession because of that. Many of those who pursue coaching may do so because of the influence of their youth coach. Every adult who chooses to serve, teach, and mentor students must know why they do what they do. What motivates you to work with students? Simon Sinek introduced the golden circle concept in *Start with Why* (2011). The outer circle is what we do (teach, coach, direct), the middle circle is how we do it (plan, execute, reflect). The center, golden circle is our why (purpose, cause, or belief). Taking time to reflect on past experiences, beliefs, and values can help crystalize and retain your why. If you don't know your *why*, you will lose your *way* and your students will suffer.

Build Character: Recognize that student performances, records, or successes are one thing, but who they become as people as a result of their time with you is equally or even *more* important. Character contributes to a society of people with integrity, courage, honesty, and loyalty, which builds essential trust among people that is necessary for success in all relationships.

Take people as they are: Accept that people will disappoint you. They won't practice as hard as you think they should, they won't know their lines in the timeframe you establish, and they may not carry themselves on the court in the manner you expect. Love, trust, and forgive them anyway.

Build the team: Relationships among the team, cast, or group will be the root of their success or failure. Be intentional to create opportunities to build camaraderie among the cast and teammates. When you attend the end-of-season banquets, team dinners, or drama award ceremonies, it is crystal clear which adults have simply done the job and those who have developed trusting relationships by the way the students respond to and speak about the impact the adult leaders had on them and their peers.

Establish norms/expectations: Has your football team, musical cast, or dance team established group norms? Are members taught what norms are and are they included in creating them for the group? Is time set aside to teach them how to uphold the norms? Much like the classroom, coaches and directors should outline expectations they have, allow students to establish their own rules, and blend them in a way that allows them to become norms or agreements.

Teach, *always* teach: Yelling doesn't help...anything. Take for example the coach who calls a timeout and yells, berates, and lambastes their players. You can witness this anywhere from youth sports to collegiate games. The next time you witness this, watch the interaction and the performance of the players immediately out of the timeout. The young brain, in general, does not respond well to screaming, yelling, or belittling. As the coach is using the timeout to lash out while simultaneously screaming instructions for the play right out of the timeout, be assured that the only thing the player hears and feels is, "Coach is angry. Coach is mad at me. I better not mess up. I don't want to be singled out." The young brain does not hear corrective measures; it hears anger. Those players rarely hear a word about the play that has been called. Invariably, players go out and fail to execute what the coach just directed them to do in the timeout and the coach gets upset (again) with the players. In such instances, the coach has failed to teach.

Practice self-regulation: A coach's poor self-regulation impacts the performance of her players. Some of the most successful coaches, at nearly every level, have tremendous self-regulation and enough insight, awareness, and maturity to know when they need to check themselves. As leaders, we have to make sure our coaches, directors, and sponsors know they can raise expectations without raising their voices or the level of fear. The young brain will respond much better to teaching, directing, and encouraging than yelling, blaming, and ridiculing. The stage, court, or field are an extension of the classroom. Teach them.

Build leadership capacity: Does the coach always have to be the one talking in a timeout? Can a student director get as much or more out of their peers as the adult director? When it comes to expecting excellence, no one needs the title "principal" to lead in this arena. You are a leader because of your ability to inspire others, to build their confidence, to influence their thinking, and more importantly, their behavior. Young people have an amazing ability to do this with their peers when given the opportunity. Imagine how athletes would respond if the volleyball coach took a time out and directed her team to talk to each other about the performance problems on the court at that moment and have them propose solutions. They are capable of doing this when adults teach them how and believe in their ability to problem-solve and lead.

When youth sports became so dictated and controlled by adults, we lost something important. Not long ago, a good friend coached his team in the State of Iowa basketball tournament. His team did not perform to their capability and when asked why he thought that was the case, he said, "They don't know how to be leaders anymore. The adults pick the teams, make the foul calls, and holler instructions constantly at the kids. They don't go out and pick their team, call their own fouls, and coach themselves and each other. They have lost those natural opportunities to develop leadership skills." As a result, teachers, coaches, and directors must integrate opportunities for students to use their leadership capacity—but they must first have it themselves.

An Activities Director recently shared the following with a fellow administrator:

> We have far too many technical fouls called on our coach, players, and bench. I think my coach doesn't handle himself very well. He gets worked up easily over officials' calls. From the time the ball is tipped into the air, my coach is on the officials. He yells, throws his jacket, stomps his feet, and waves his hands in the air on every call he disagrees with and it gets the kids and the fans reacting the same way.

The scenario is pinging with red flags about the coach's maturity and emotional intelligence. The line between "passion" and "problematic" is pretty thin here. At the heart of an emotionally intelligent person is self-awareness. Through his body language, jacket throwing, yelling at players during timeouts, and stomping his feet, the coach models an inability to self-regulate. A coach's inability to self-regulate rubs off on his players. In this instance, what you model is what you get—excessive technicals. If the coach were able to use his emotions in a manner that encouraged and inspired his team, the crowd, or even himself, the experience of the players, parents, community, and even the coach himself would be entirely different. It begs the question, "Why has the coach been allowed to behave this way?" This scenario is as much a failure of leadership as it is the failure of the coach. The activities director was either unwilling or unable to address the coach's behavior and, given that he shared this situation to get help from a colleague, we suspect it is the latter. Perhaps you have heard the phrase, "What you permit, you promote." In this case, the principal had tolerated the coach's antics, and players, parents, and officials had come to expect that behavior from the coach. The activities director should have candidly addressed the coach's behavior from a place of care and concern.

This scenario illustrates the need for building administrators to work closely with those whom they supervise. Oftentimes, activity director positions are entry level positions into school administration and, therefore, can benefit from coaching and modeling from their principal. Additionally, developing interview questions that reveal the degree to which a candidate manages, reflects, and receives feedback is critical to the hiring process. As leaders, what questions are we asking candidates as part of the interview process? Do we ask questions around maturity? Self-management? Modeling behavior?

Some questions to consider when interviewing coaches and directors:

+ Why do you want to be a coach (director)?
+ What experiences have you had that prepared you to lead a team (cast or ensemble)?
+ Describe your understanding of effective coaching? What is it and how does it look during practice?
+ What do you find most difficult about coaching (directing)?
+ What measures do you use to determine your effectiveness as a coach (director)?
+ Describe a time when a player (or performer) frustrated you. How did you handle it?

These sample questions are designed to gain an understanding of the candidate's "why." The questions also give a sense of the candidate's maturity and self-regulation. While the perceptions of the candidate are important, equally important in the hiring process is getting feedback about these areas from reference checks. Asking others, for example, to tell you a time the candidate was frustrated with a situation and how he responded will give you insight into their emotional regulation.

A word on reference checks: It's astonishing the number of employees who have applied, interviewed, and were offered a position in another district without a single reference check with a current or previous employer. This is not only unprofessional, but it is also dangerous. Historically, reference checks were used to ensure that a candidate had the experience, education, and qualifications they professed to have, but times have changed. In addition to classroom teachers, school leaders must reflect on their hiring practices related to coaches, directors, and sponsors. Excellence in our schools extends beyond the classroom and excellence in our hiring practices must as well. Reference checks, done properly, will provide prospective employers with the information they need to make a hiring decision.

These inquiries also provide insight into ways a new employer can best support a new staff member. Questions like, "What is the best way to give feedback to the candidate?" or "How does the candidate respond to feedback?" provide invaluable insight as to how to bring out the best in a new team member. Questions such as, "In what way is your organization better because of this person?" "Do the candidate's students and colleagues trust them? How do you know?" will give insight into their ability to influence and relate with others. Any information that provides feedback on the way a candidate will contribute to your school culture is beneficial. If reference checks are skipped or glossed over, there is potential for an unforeseen situation that will hurt you and your institution.

To hire someone without conducting reference checks is professional malpractice in two ways. First, when a new hire learns that their new employer never even took the time to consult references, it runs the risk of sending the message that this hiring process was inadequate at best and lazy at worst. Second, should that new hire do or say something that brings damage to your school's reputation or the safety and well-being of your students, you might as well start writing the settlement checks. It is incumbent upon you to do your due diligence and conduct reference checks on every prospective employee.

In *Emotional Intelligence* (1995), Goleman explains that emotional intelligence is more than just being nice. At strategic times, according to Goleman, we are called to engage in conversations designed to directly address a consequential truth that we or others are avoiding because it is uncomfortable.

In an effort to be nice or non-confrontational, what consequential truth have you been avoiding? Who needs some feedback from you that you have difficulty delivering? Addressing and confronting are two different things. Have you ever dealt with a staff member or student who interacted with another person and the outcome was pretty negative? Invariably, the staff member or student says, "I just confronted her (him) about it." In other words, they were challenging the other person, most likely in a curt, maybe even hostile, manner. When one person "confronts" another, nothing good comes of it. The "confrontation" usually centers around some sort of (un)truth: "I heard she said this about me." Or, "I think he took something from me, so I confronted him."

When school leaders think they have to "confront" a person or situation, the level of discomfort rises, but if the school leader considers it feedback or coaching, anxiety diminishes. Teachers give feedback, parents share a perspective, and spouses have a point of view. Unfortunately, "confronting" can easily dissolve into chastising and berating—neither of which is productive or helpful. Even worse than "confronting" is when people say, "Can I be brutally honest with you?" Unfortunately, people sometimes lead with being more brutal than honest when they ask this. Depending on the size and administrative structure of a school, what if the principal/activities director initiated a conversation with the coach who doesn't manage himself well that went something like this:

> Administrator: "Coach, can I give you some feedback?"
> Coach: "Sure."

No one feels threatened by "feedback" like they would when someone asks if they can be "brutally honest." By asking permission to offer feedback, the coach has now permitted you to share your thoughts with him.

> *Administrator: I have been struggling to have this conversation with you. As I look at the feedback we get from officials, watch the conduct of our players, and witness the unruly behavior of fans, I have started to notice that the way you manage yourself impacts the reactions of others. When you raise your hands in the air upset at an official's call, your players also start to protest calls which leads to the fans becoming disgruntled. I share some of the blame for this. If I had been paying more attention or had been more willing to have this conversation earlier, we probably wouldn't be where we are now. That is on me and I am sorry I didn't sit down with you sooner. Now that we both know better, we must both do better. I am going to ask you to manage yourself better along the bench. I want to help you meet the expectations of our school by encouraging you to conduct yourself in a way that represents the expectations of all adults in this school. Please explain to your players, much like I have explained to you, that you haven't been holding them to the standard expected of our students. I want to be clear that the way our basketball program has been representing our school must change. How can I help and support you to get us back to representing our school values and what you told me your program would be about when I hired you?"*

How do you think the coach would respond to this feedback? The fact that the administrator owns his role in the situation would certainly help. Furthermore, the administrator acknowledged avoiding the conversation and he assumed responsibility for that. Finally, the administrator asks the coach how he can support him to get their team back to representing their school in a desirable fashion. In this way, the principal has made his expectations of the coach and players clear. He has also communicated his role in the situation and his willingness to lend support. Are there conversations like this that you need to be having? When was the last time you had an uncomfortable conversation? Please know the angst you are carrying just thinking about having the conversation is far worse than actually talking to the staff member who needs the feedback. What are you waiting for?

The Influence Of Affluence On School Activities

In 2015, Texas teenager, Ethan Couch, was sentenced to rehabilitation and ten years' probation after driving drunk and killing four people. His story made national news when a witness for his defense argued the teen suffered from "affluenza"—the result of wealthy, privileged parents who never set limits. The affluenza defense and the seemingly lenient consequence was met with outrage. While this is an extreme example, "affluenza" is not a new concept and certainly not limited to criminal proceedings. Authors Graaf, Wann & Naylor (2014) challenge readers to consider how over-consumption is impacting society, suggesting instead, "...that it is possible to build a society based on *not more but better, not selfishness but sharing, not a competition but community.*" (2014, p. 130).

Parents everywhere spend weekend after weekend traveling to tournaments and spending more time on the road than their homes. Youth sports has taken on a life of its own, and while the benefits of being part of a team are tremendous, we struggle with the youth sports culture because it is becoming increasingly and inherently an unequal playing field—starting at very young ages.

Aside from the insane amount of time, travel, and resources thrown into youth sports, the reality is that youth sports has become less about cultivating and developing skills and talents in all youth and more about affluence: for children of parents who can afford team fees, travel, hotel, food, coach fees, uniforms, athletic bags, tournament admission fees and private lessons. In essence, youth participation in sports has become a tremendous opportunity *for those of means*. For parents choosing between gas in their car or food on the table, organized youth sports is rarely an option. There is a very real and detrimental opportunity gap related to youth sports. A gap exists in dance, music, art, and academics as well. The results are that those with financial means are inherently likely to be the cream that rises to the top. Many young people are either thriving in youth opportunities or suffering without. There is a very real and detrimental opportunity gap related to youth sports...Many young people are either thriving in youth opportunities or suffering without.

> There is a very real and detrimental opportunity gap related to youth sports...Many young people are either thriving in youth opportunities or suffering without.

In his book, *Dream Hoarders* (2018), the economist Richard Reeves writes that economic mobility in the U.S. has been spiraling downward in part because of "opportunity hoarding." This same concept applies to the downward trend of youth participation in sports, at least among those with limited financial means. Parents of children as young as eight years old are jockeying to get their child on a traveling athletic team and they are willing to pay big bucks to make it happen. In doing so, the system ends up knocking out other eight-year-olds who do not come from families with the same level of financial resources. The sad truth is that many high schools have incredible athletes roaming their halls but their single parent or financially-strapped family could not afford to get them on the traveling team and those athletes simply give up, knowing they will not have the same opportunity to compete. The "opportunity hoarding" isn't confined just to athletics either. Competitive parenting has resulted in parents going to great (even illegal) lengths to pull all sorts of privilege maneuvers to get their child into the elementary, high school, or college of choice, to land competitive internships or jobs, or to seal that academic or athletic scholarship. The college admission scandals in 2019 (Medina, Benner & Taylor, 2019) illustrate how wealthy people schemed to use their privilege to ensure their children were admitted to elite colleges and universities.

Youth sports have value in our society—the relationships children forge with coaches, teammates, and athletes from schools and clubs are tremendous. The lessons of teamwork, commitment, and self-discipline are invaluable. While it is good and right to support and encourage our children in their passions and goals, are we inadvertently contributing to a culture that knocks children as young as eight years old out of the competition because their parents cannot afford to participate? Does your school struggle with knowing there are families with only one vehicle and this prevents them from dedicating the time to running their kids to/from practices and competitions? Is it difficult as a teacher or leader knowing there are tremendous athletes, musicians, and artists with incredible talent walking the hallways but they are not on our courts, fields, or stage because they weren't able to participate? The same can be said about speech/debate, drama, and academics. Schools, families, and communities have a responsibility to provide every child the chance to participate and succeed. The "haves" accrue more in every arena; the "have nots" have less. Are we comfortable with this?

The Coach And The Critic

One of the most challenging aspects of coaching or directing students is the expectation level of the student and their parents—and they often do not match. Coaches and directors can expect a level of frustration and disappointment regarding playing time, a role a student didn't get in the play, or the solo that went to someone else in the upcoming concert. Some of this disappointment comes internally from the students; however, the resentment and disappointment with the student's role in an activity often come from a parent. We have all heard the coach who says, "Coaching would be great if it didn't involve parents." The stress and tension coaches and directors feel when it comes to parents is not likely to go away; however, recognizing that parents are an integral piece to the success of student opportunities is an important realization. Those in charge of student programs need to balance parental support for student programs with the coach or director's desires regarding the goals of their programs. As stated earlier, parents not only have the right, but they also have an obligation to advocate for their child when it comes to the classroom experience. The same is true for school programs.

Coaches, directors, and sponsors can take steps to mitigate disappointments that invariably surface through school programs while also maximizing the experience for their students and families.

EYES ON CULTURE IN ACTION

Form positive relationships: When students trust adults, they may be disappointed they aren't in the role they saw themselves in, but they don't question the motives or intent of the adults leading them. Cultivating positive, caring relationships with school program participants diminishes suspicion about favoritism and adult motives that erode trust and confidence.

Focus on building a team: At the heart of healthy teams is honesty. Are the coaches and directors at your school having honest conversations with their players and performers about the role they see for themselves and the role the coaches and directors see them having? Are coaches, directors, and sponsors making time and creating opportunities for student connection?

Connect with parents and families: Although extracurricular activities are designed for students, we can't underestimate how important these events are to their families as well. Reach out to parents, introduce yourself by way of an email, text, or short video. Call a parent or guardian early on to express what a valued member their child is to the team, cast, club, or ensemble.

Engage with parents/guardians: Ask them to write one measurable goal they have for their child for the upcoming season. This will help gauge the reality of their assessment and prepare you if the goal they have for their child is not reasonable or achievable.

Solicit feedback from parents/guardians: It is the parents of the athletes or performers who likely have the best pulse regarding their child's experience with a school program. They are the experts about their children and getting their input about what motivates or aggravates their child as well as the most effective ways the coach or director can best support the participant is valuable information.

Be organized: It is imperative that every practice, rehearsal, or meeting is mapped out just like a lesson for the classroom. Provide a schedule to students and parents so everyone can plan and prepare. Families are living busy lives and they need this information early and often to make plans for the entire family. Have an established communication schedule (every Monday, for example) that involves a brief message with pertinent information for parents: upcoming schedule, cast picture date, team mealtime, and more.

Start and end on time: If the schedule you provide states rehearsal ends at 5:00 p.m., your performers should be walking out of the building by 5:01 p.m. Keeping students after the bell rings at the end of the day is wrong and so is keeping students involved in extracurricular activities past the scheduled end time. Younger students are dependent on rides from parents while older students often drive themselves. When you keep students later than the expected end time, the parents picking their child up are irritated when they come out late, and the parents of those students who drive start to worry about their safety when they don't walk through the doors at the anticipated time. Either scenario will alienate parents.

Give feedback to all participants: To culturize student activities, instill confidence in all participants. Find and communicate a role for all members. When an athlete or performer has one set of expectations for their role and the coach or director has a different set, confusion, hurt, and resentment will follow. If you want to reduce division among the participants, make sure you coach and give feedback to all participants, not just the starters or leads.

Set a good example: Students take their cues from adults. Coaches and directors must model the behaviors they expect. Be positive, be loyal, and accept feedback from participants and their parents. Above all, relate with your participants in safe, supportive, and predictable ways.

The Coach	The Critic
Consistent	Unpredictable
Fosters Cooperation	Creates Division
Sets a good example	Behaves immaturely
Recognizes non-verbals	Indifferent
Trusted for their judgment	Questioned for their judgment
Encourage openness and input	My way or the highway
Nurture relationships	Manipulate participants
Value participants as people	Values participants for their results
Predictable	Impulsive
Consistent emotions	Irrational
Fosters growth environment	Fosters fear environment
Inspires participants	Deflates participants

Because I Said So

A friend recently completed an advanced education degree. What initially was an effort to earn the superintendent certification quickly became about much more. Jim was informed by the university graduate program that he could complete the superintendent's program but if he wanted to earn the educational specialist degree (Ed.S.) he would need to take the Graduate Record Exam (GRE) for admission to the program. When Jim realized he would only need an additional twelve credit hours for both the superintendent's certification and the Ed.S. degree, he decided to pursue admission; however, the GRE requirement rubbed Jim wrong for several reasons and he expressed his misgivings in a thoughtful, respectful email that outlined the reasons for his concern. His chief objection was that the GRE is a predictor of someone's ability to complete graduate course work. Having already completed a master's degree in educational leadership combined with several years of administrative experience at that time, Jim believed that his previous graduate work had already been evaluated and successfully demonstrated. Jim's thoughtful email went without a response for a significant time, so he sent another. In that email, Jim offered to speak with anyone from the education department and travel from out of town to the campus to discuss the matter in person. Jim received a one-line response from the head of the department:

Hi Jim,
   We are standing by our admissions requirements.

Jim was stunned. An educational professional with a stellar career in school administration had received a response that was tantamount to, "Because we said so." Jim said he wanted to reply, "I feel like you're sort of on the fence on this issue." Instead, he chose to file a complaint with the university ombudsperson, who responded to his complaint within a couple of days, informing Jim that the education department incorrectly applied the graduate college admissions requirements in his case. The path had been paved for Jim to proceed with completing the degree. To this day, Jim remains disappointed that no one from the graduate program ever picked up the phone and called him, if for no other reason than to treat him like a professional and to better understand his perspective. And they certainly could have done so after it was discovered their process was faulty. Jim finished the program and moved on, but it was an experience that caused him to pause. As a teacher and coach, Jim shared that this experience prompted him to ask himself some important, reflective questions. Jim wondered if he treated his students that way? Do they feel shot down before they even have a chance to share their perspective? How approachable was he when people disagreed with his team's policies or expectations? Are there former students or players who never felt they had a voice with Jim as a result of the "Because I said so" experiences they had with him? Jim made a list of ways he could widen the circle of input and leadership by eliminating the "Because I said so" response:

Establish classroom/team norms: Jim created opportunities for students and players to have a direct say in the culture of their environments. He set time aside for students to collaboratively establish norms for how they would operate as a group. He made posters of those norms and hung them in the classroom and locker room so students had a constant visual reminder of the agreements established among them.

Get clear about expectations *and* the reason behind them: Students will not do what you do not expect and they cannot meet your expectations if you do not teach them. Announcing expectations without models for how the expectations look or sound in specific environments will lead to confusion and frustration. Adding to this further will be proclamations made without providing any logic behind the expectations. Again, clarity precedes competence.

Choose sincerity over sarcasm: The word "sarcasm" stems from the Greek word "sarkasmos", meaning "to tear flesh, bite the lips in rage, sneer." People who think sarcasm is funny may want to think again. A little sarcasm goes a long way—and can do a lot of damage in the process. Teachers, coaches, and directors serve as sources of encouragement, and sarcasm risks damaging the established trusting relationships and creating insecurity for others. Honest and sincere words of encouragement and affirmation are always the better option.

A principal friend, Anne, relayed an interaction she had with her new school superintendent. As part of his inaugural speech to district administrators, the superintendent made clear that he expected administrators to speak up if they disagreed with him. In a bit of a gruff tone, he said, "Do not sit on your hands. If you have a problem or disagree, I better hear it from you first."

Anne explained that she found it difficult and uncomfortable to give her new boss feedback. She felt he interrupted her or would cut her off mid-thought. Other administrators were feeling that way as well, but who was going to tell him? On one occasion while she was sitting in his office, the new superintendent was making a decision regarding seniors and graduation during the COVID-19 pandemic. He finished the conversation by saying, "Anne, if you think my idea is a horseshit idea, then tell me it's a horseshit idea." Anne quickly thought about how apprehensive she had felt about giving feedback to her new boss and said, "I don't think it's a horseshit idea, but can I share something with you?" The new boss nodded affirmatively and Anne proceeded, "We don't know each other very well yet, but I need you to know that I find it difficult to give you feedback. I often feel you cut me off mid-sentence or shoot down an idea before I've had the opportunity to fully explain it. I know you want us to give you feedback, but I just needed to tell you that I don't feel you make it very easy to do so."

Anne said her new boss stared straight at her. She later mused, "I felt like he was staring straight through my soul." Anne's new boss was quiet for a minute then said, "Shame on me. Shame on me for making you feel that way. I appreciate you telling me this." Anne quickly said, "I didn't say that to shame you. I just needed to register with you how I feel, so that, moving forward, I can feel more comfortable and confident in giving you the feedback I know you expect us to give." Anne never again wondered or questioned whether she should speak up. Kudos to Anne. Despite her concerns about speaking up, she did, but double kudos to Anne's new boss. He could have easily dismissed her perspective or said something to make Anne feel embarrassed or uncomfortable. Instead, his words were an excellent way to model self-reflection. "Shame on me" sent a strong signal to Anne that:

The new boss truly wanted feedback, even if it didn't feel like he did. If we truly want effective relationships rooted in trust and communication, we must be willing to speak up. When was the last time you gave a colleague, parent, or supervisor feedback you were reluctant to give? What type of feedback are you withholding from someone else because of your apprehension about how it will be received?

Openness invariably pays off: Despite Anne's hesitation to give her honest assessment to her new boss, doing so paved the way for what she reported as newfound confidence in sharing other thoughts.

The new boss modeled two key leadership traits: listening and ownership. He listened to what Anne said, briefly reflected, and took ownership of his role in her apprehension. In doing so, he validated Anne's feelings but also signaled how important it is to honor the role of each person, regardless of title.

In the movie, *Remember the Titans*, one scene depicts Coach Boone walking his football field on a cold night. He says, "Aaaaahhh...this is my sanctuary." Do our performers view the field, court, deck, or stage as their sanctuary? A sanctuary is a place of refuge or safety. It is a place of security and safekeeping. How do you boost your sanctuary? What are the tones being used with players, casts, and student groups? How do the coaches and directors communicate with their students? How are conversations crafted so the feedback is coaching in nature, not ridiculing or criticizing? How can you know if the sport you coach or the play you direct is a sanctuary for your athletes and performers? There are a few tell-tale signs:

Tone among the team: Are the students playful with one another? Do they seem to enjoy each other and share a common goal? Do their faces reflect joy or compliance?

Team feedback: Can the teammates and castmates work through issues, challenges, and conflicts without adults providing the direction? Healthy experiences can be heard in the voices of players and performers giving feedback to each other.

Ownership for mistakes: When participants can say, "That is my fault" or "I was wrong" it builds trust and encourages healthy risk-taking. Assuming ownership makes for stronger teammates.

Another poignant scene from *Remember the Titans* is when co-captain Gerry Bertier tells his co-captain, Julius Campbell, that he has the strength and skills to run over anyone on the field but that he doesn't work well with others, so he's not as effective. Gerry tried to get Julius to understand that he needs to be a better teammate. Julius responds angrily that "there is no team" and saying he's just there to "get" his and take care of himself. Gerry responds, "Now, that's the worst attitude to have." Julius shoots right back, "Attitude reflects leadership, Captain." *Attitude reflects leadership.* What kind of attitude do our coaches and directors have with our students?

EYES ON CULTURE IN ACTION

Effective communication: People often focus on one's ability to speak or write articulately as a measure of effective communication. Effective listening is a skill that is often overshadowed, but listening is one of the most effective communication tools. Can your players come to you to register concerns or disappointments?

Trust: Do your students know that your word is golden? Creating conditions for students to trust a coach or director, trust the process, and trust the feedback provided is essential to a positive experience. Holding all members of the team accountable to the same standard is one path to building trust. So, too, is acknowledging mistakes and failures. When adults do this, it makes the path for students to do so that much easier.

Placing blame: Win or lose, effective coaches avoid placing blame on their athletes. When the production on opening night does not go as well as anticipated, the director who expects excellence will talk about us, we, and I—not you.

Team building: Establishing trusting relationships with every member of the team is the path to an excellent student opportunity. If you are the head coach or director, start by developing a process to build your team of adults who will coach and direct your students. Make clear what type of culture and environment you want everyone to operate from and promote.

Clarify roles: Meet with each player/performer/member to better know who they are, what they value, and how they see their role. Have a director's discussion with cast members to understand why the production is important to them and what they can contribute. These conversations are also fertile ground to share with the athlete or performer how you will support them, why you value them, and what you need from them to create a team rooted in trust in pursuit of excellence.

No more "Because I said so": Drop "Because I said so." Drop it from your vocabulary; drop it from your demeanor. Nurture an atmosphere that encourages students to provide input. Create conditions that encourage students to bring forward concerns about the experience they and their peers are having with your program.

Follow through: One of the most rewarding aspects of working with and coaching others is being able to hear other voices when we work through difficult or less-than-ideal situations. When we avoid, deny, or fail to follow up, we are sending a clear message about our culture: Your voice does not matter. No one wants to be a part of any organization or activity that rejects their opinions, experiences, and ideas.

Can We Talk About This?

A high school principal received a call from an angry parent who relayed that she believed the high school theater director was retaliating against her daughter since she decided against auditioning for the spring play. The parent gave some examples that made her daughter feel slighted: The director wouldn't look at or talk to the student in the hallway. She heard from others that the director had talked about her negatively to other theater students. Other theater students had started treating the student differently by actively excluding her. The principal asked if the student had talked to the director about this. The mother responded, "She hasn't talked to the director since she emailed him to let him know she was quitting theater. He never even had the decency to respond." The principal followed up with the director. He acknowledged receiving the email from the student and sheepishly admitted he did not respond to her, noting that her parents had been difficult to deal with and, if the student didn't want to be there, he wasn't going to beg her to stay.

When students decide to quit an activity or program, how the adults respond reveals a great deal about the culture established. In this scenario, imagine how the student felt when the theater director did not respond, let alone even acknowledge receiving her email. One could certainly make the case that the student should not have communicated the message about quitting through email. We agree, but it also begs the question as to what has been taught and modeled to students about time, place, and manner when it comes to communicating with the director (coach, teacher, administrator). When students see adults every day at school but choose to email instead of speaking to us, there has to be some reflection about how approachable those students view us. When athletes have another team member tell the coach that they quit, how should the coach respond? Far too often, adults take the path of least resistance and simply move on without any follow up with the athlete who quit or their parents/guardians. Students give up when they don't feel valued. When adults do not reach out, follow up, and respond to students who quit, it confirms for them that they never really were a valued member of the team. This is a culture killer signal to that participant and the rest of the team.

EYES ON CULTURE IN ACTION

Separate a child from their parent: Regardless of how burdensome it can be to deal with a difficult parent, responding negatively or not at all to a student is a quick path to destroying a positive culture or a future relationship. No adult should respond negatively to a child based on the behavior of that student's parents.

Respond to student communications: When staff and administration fail to respond to a communication, students and parents will make up stories in their minds about why there was no response or the motivation behind the silence and it rarely reflects positive intent on your part. A situation that began with a student feeling disrespected and devalued quickly becomes an opportunity for the parent to act defensively and with hostility.

There is no shortcut to integrity: Consider how this situation might have played out if the director had responded to the student's email this way: "I am so sorry to hear you want to quit theater. Can we talk about this? I would like to meet with you and a parent, if possible, to talk about what led you to this decision." The principal would likely have never received that parent phone call and complaint. If we expect excellence from our student-athletes and performers, we must be willing to have honest conversations and be willing to listen to others about their experience in our programs. When this doesn't happen, the student leaves feeling dejected, betrayed, disrespected, and embarrassed.

Inviting is not begging: By inviting the students to discuss their concerns, the door remains open. If the student chooses to close it, fine, but adults should not slam the door on student participation because they don't want to "beg." Remember, we are dealing with young people, with young brains—they need help and support navigating this type of situation, particularly when they are wounded.

The Power Of Words

In Don Miguel Ruiz's *The Four Agreements* (1997), one of the agreements is to "be impeccable with your word." "Impeccable" comes from the Latin *impeccabilis*, meaning: not to sin. Being impeccable with your word is an agreement, but sounds more like a command. It is the kind of command that requires you to be intentional in the words you use toward others in times of joy, anger, despair, and frustration. Who among us has not said something we wish we could suck right back in? As teachers, leaders, parents, partners, and friends, our words matter to those who hear them, but in many cases, we may not have just the right words for others. There were no "right" words for Jack that day he shared that his dad had killed his mom, and then himself. Sometimes the less we say, the more sufficient their impact. When a parent registers that their child felt embarrassed by your words, apologize. It doesn't matter whether you agree with how the child feels or if that was your intent; what matters is that you acknowledge the hurt and say, "I'm sorry."

Years ago a staff member shared that her daughter, Abbie, was struggling with her new 3rd-grade teacher. Abbie, who ordinarily loved school, loved learning, and loved her teachers, was now complaining of stomach aches, asking to stay home, and engaging in other school avoidance behaviors. One day Abbie came blasting out of school, got in the car, slouched into the seat, and started bawling. Her mother asked her what was wrong, but the daughter was inconsolable. After several minutes, Abbie finally yelled, "Mrs. Jones likes to embarrass and humiliate students!"

Later, during a meeting with the teacher, Abbie bravely told her how uncomfortable she felt when Mrs. Jones singled students out. She told Mrs. Jones that she didn't like it when she sounded mean towards classmates. Mrs. Jones responded by telling Abbie that she appreciated her talking to her about it and that she would never want any student to feel that way. Once they exited, Abbie said, "She's fake, Mom. She doesn't talk like that to us. She just sounded all sweet to you because you are an adult." The situation did not improve, so the mother scheduled a meeting with the principal, Mr. Moser, who talked at great length about how eight-year-olds have different perceptions about situations. He was uncomfortable with the conversation and offered to move Abbie to another class but asked the parents not to say anything to others because he would "have a mass exodus on my hands."

Abbie's mom retorted, "I guess the eight-year old's perception is pretty accurate after all."

In this scenario, Abbie never felt like she could go to Mrs. Jones for help, comfort, or support—and neither did any other student. Imagine if Mr. Moser had addressed Mrs. Jones previously when other parents registered the same concerns. If he had brought the concerns to Mrs. Jones, saying, "This is the feedback I am getting and it tells me there is a culture problem in your classroom. You have been a valued teacher here and I do not want your reputation to take a hit. Parents talk to other parents and a reputation will build that I won't be able to help you with and from which you may never recover. The complaints will continue unless and until the experience of other children in your classroom is different. What do you think we need to do about it?"

Leaders often avoid difficult conversations because they don't want to hurt the feelings of others. In reality, people often delay or skip challenging conversations to avoid their own discomfort. Imagine how exhausting the situation became for Mr. Moser as a result of his avoidance. There are a lot of Mrs. Joneses in our classrooms and as many Mr. Mosers leading schools. If we want our students to grow and achieve at the highest levels, they must feel physically and emotionally safe in the classroom and the school. How can you tell if students feel that way in your school?

EYES ON CULTURE IN ACTION

Students name the adults: Students in safe and supportive schools can identify one adult in the building they could go to if they were in trouble or having trouble. When you meet with students about their behavior or personal matters, ask them if they have an adult in the building they can go to. If more students cannot identify a staff member than those who can, there's a culture problem and excellence cannot grow there.

Words from the adults are uplifting: Educators (and parents) must be aware of how important words are and the impact they have on children. Be mindful of the intentions behind your words. Is what (and how) you are saying helping or hurting the student? Is what you are saying something that needs to be said and are you the best person to deliver the message? Know when you have the connection and when someone else has a better connection.

Time, place, and manner is considered: When, where, and how adults talk to students (and others) about issues is as important, if not more, as the conversation itself. When talking to students about anything ranging from student performance to behavior or personal concerns, we must ask ourselves the following: Is this the appropriate time to have this conversation? Is this the appropriate place to talk about this matter? Am I conducting myself in a manner that will make this exchange positive and productive? Time, place, and manner matter.

Adults keep their word: Adults who keep their word with students build a foundation of trust. Can you trust or respect someone who doesn't keep their word? Likely not. Neither can students.

Students get a fresh start: When students have missteps, do they feel like they are forever judged, or do they feel they get a fresh start with teachers, coaches, or administrators? When meeting with students after they have made a mistake, it is imperative to tell students that the matter is over, no one is going to hold it over their head, and they have a fresh start. Once you tell them this, it is important to follow up by saying, "Do you believe me when I say this to you?"

CHAPTER 4

Core Principle 3:
Carry the Banner -
Culturizing School Pride

In *Culturize*, readers were challenged to consider strategies to respond to those in our organizations who talk negatively about others or the institution and to identify culture builders and address culture killers related to this. Every organization has the naysayers, the "What about?" and the "We've always done it this way" members. The challenge is to bring those people along in a supportive way while simultaneously insulating the positive, innovative, and hopeful ones. Imagine if students and staff at your school carried the school banner in the community much like an Olympian who carries the banner for their country at the opening and closing ceremonies. Would they mirror the pride, joy, and honor exuded by the Olympians? Would it be a different experience for students than it would be for staff?

Culturizing school pride requires a focus and attention on all members of the school community—students, staff, families, and community members. Modeling positive interactions sends the message about how school leaders want students and staff to talk to and treat each other. What we model is far more effective than simply telling others how we want them to act. Every interaction with a student, staff member, parent, or community member is an opportunity for that individual to experience a connection to their school that will determine the manner in which they carry the banner—negatively or positively, once they leave.

School leaders are not and cannot be perfect in every interaction, but school community members generally have a sense of their school leaders and the type of people and leaders they are. There will always be the outliers—the ones who love you regardless of your mistakes and the ones who will never like you no matter your contributions. In general, though, the community as a whole knows what type of leader they have at the helm. School members know which leaders ask people to do things they are unwilling to do themselves. They know who blames others and who assumes responsibility. They know which school leaders are committed to serving others and which are merely doing a job.

School members also know when their leaders genuinely care about them and their well-being. They know they can go to their leader with their joys or sorrows, regardless of their role in the organization. When leaders treat people with respect and compassion, they are modeling the type of connection that makes others forever proud to be associated with the school as a student, teacher, or parent and it starts with relationships. The quality of relationships determines the quality of your school and the quality of your school culture. Culture is built with every interaction, communication, policy, and practice of a school. If we want students, staff, and parents to carry the banner of our schools, leaders must focus on a systematic approach that ensures all community members embrace the tone, know and accept the standards, promote an inclusive community, and operate from a place of honor and integrity—in good times and in bad.

Leaders Set the Tone And the Boundaries

School pride starts the minute a new student, family, or staff member steps foot on the campus. Whether it is to register for school or interview for an open position, how these potential school community members feel about joining our school starts with how we greet and engage them. At the heart of a positive school culture resides a secretary who helps set the tone about our schools. If this is not true for your school, you may want to reconsider who is in your secretary role. Does your secretary sound welcoming and hospitable or crabby and dismissive? Does your secretary treat others with a helpful spirit or as a tolerated interruption? Do your students and staff members avoid certain offices so as not to deal with a certain secretary? If you answered yes to any of these questions, you have people in place who are unable or unwilling to carry the banner for your school and, as school leaders, we have a responsibility to either counsel them out or coach them up. Consider the following story Jimmy experienced on a school visit:

> As I drove up to the school, a banner the size of a semi-truck jumped out at me. It was hanging above the main entrance to the school and it read, "School of Excellence!" To say I was jazzed to visit the school was an understatement. I had heard many wonderful things about this elementary school and I couldn't wait to soak it all in. After all, I love learning from others and seeing excellence at work.
>
> I walked into the main office and approached a long wooden counter that went from wall to wall. Off to my right was a young man standing there looking through his mail. The office staff, three in all, were sitting at their desks. I found it unusual that not a

single one of them greeted me, stood up to approach me, or at the very least, acknowledged my presence. I could hear the one closest to me gossiping about another staff member. Although I couldn't hear the two furthest away from me, I could see the body language of one of them who was on the phone and it didn't exude positivity. I remember thinking the conversation she was having was annoying her, especially after I saw the eye roll she aimed at her colleague next to her. Suddenly, I heard a voice, "Do you need something?" asked the person closest to me. "Yes, I am here to see the principal. I have an appointment," I responded. "Take a seat and I will give him the message." No, How are you? May I tell him who is here? Can I get you some water? Nothing. Just take a seat. And so I did. I had just sat down when a young boy (I later found out he was in 3rd grade) came into the office and sat next to me. I could tell he was upset about something. "Hi there. I like your shoes. They are cool," I said. He looked up at me and in a quiet voice he said, "Thank you; you are nice." "Thank you. You are welcome," I responded. The young man who had been going through his mail turned and started to leave. As he walked by, he stopped, looked down, and said, 'What did you do now Arturo?" And just like that, I thought to myself, "Hmmm….school of excellence?"

Scenarios like this play out each day in schools across the country. If you have ever experienced such interactions you know that sinking feeling in your gut when you walk out of an office, classroom, or building not feeling valued or appreciated. Or when you observe an interaction that leaves you heartbroken, at a loss for words, and in some cases, angry. How is this possible? What happened to a school that hung a banner proclaiming their excellence? How did it end up back in average—and at this moment, below average? It's another reminder that we are all responsible for the culture and climate of our schools, regardless of the position that we hold.

It is quite likely that the staff at this elementary school never realized how their behavior was impacting the school culture. Their actions were never intended to cause negativity within anyone who had interactions with them that morning. However, their behavior did exactly that. The teacher's comment, augmented by his tone, "What have you done *now* Arturo?" made clear that this child had been a visitor to the front office before which, unfortunately, left him stamped with a label, at least with this one teacher.

School offices must serve as sanctuaries where people can come to have their spirits boosted, not suppressed. As a space that hosts countless interactions per day, the school office atmosphere can either diminish or enhance the experiences of members of our school communities. Setting the tone begins with all of us and it is up to us to live the guiding principles that serve as a model of how we want others to be treated.

As teachers and leaders, it is our responsibility to prohibit average from becoming the standard. We must take time to reflect on and be vigilant in examining our school cultures through the eyes of the students, staff, parents, and guests we serve.

Cultivating school pride is contingent on two things:

1. *Relationships:* The members of the school community know the teachers, coaches, directors, and leaders. The community feels the school personnel knows them **and** values them as partners in the educational process. In the State of Iowa, families can open enroll children from their resident school district to another district of their choice. Schools with a poor or negative school culture are the losers in this deal. Attend student events and follow up individually with them to acknowledge their performance or efforts. Initiate conversations with students, even (especially) if you don't know their names. The size of some of our larger schools across the country impedes our ability to get

to know every student, but it shouldn't deter us from trying. When we can call students by name (and pronounce them accurately), we validate them and it tells them that we see them, we know them, and we value them. As a school principal, imagine receiving an email like this from one of your students:

> When we can call students by name (and pronounce them accurately), we validate them and it tells them that we see them, we know them, and we value them.

Dear Mrs. Kaufmann,

I'd like to thank you for coming to the drama banquet last night. However, I think it was tremendously disrespectful of you to sit in the back watching your phone the entire time you were there. I hope you understand what a serious insult that was to the people being honored. In the future, if that is your plan, please don't bother coming. Whatever it was you were looking at, I hope it was important.
Sincerely,
Matt

Now there are two ways one could look at this email. The first is how dare a student call out the principal in this way. Someone could respond defensively to an email like this and likely make the situation worse. The other way to look at this email is to consider the type of school culture that is open enough and values hearing the student voice to the extent that a student feels confident and comfortable to register his complaint with his principal. Mrs. Kaufmann has the latter perspective and responded to Matt's email with this:

Hi Matt,

Thank you for contacting me. I would like to visit with you in person about this if you have some time this week. I certainly did not intend any disrespect and would hope the support I have shown for fine arts over the years would indicate that. Unfortunately, I did have a personal situation I was trying to manage last night and it was important. In hindsight, I should have used better judgment and not attended the ceremony at all. I do like to be supportive by attending student events and simply tried to be in two places at once last night. Please accept my apology for the disrespect you felt; that was not my intention. Would you have time to visit this week to discuss further? Thank you for reaching out to me and sharing your thoughts.

Mrs. Kaufmann

What Matt did not know was that Mrs. Kaufmann had a fire at her home the day before and, unfortunately, she was texting with the insurance agent and her husband to get a restoration plan. You will notice she did not mention that to her student. Mrs. Kaufmann acknowledged both her own emotions and Matt's. Though likely a highly emotional time for Mrs. Kaufmann, she didn't make excuses or dismiss Matt's message. Offering to meet with him in person was another signal to Matt that Mrs. Kaufmann valued him and was not offended by his message.

Mrs. Kaufmann,

I'm sorry to hear that you had a personal situation; I hope everything is well. I understand how difficult it can be to juggle personal circumstances with other activities. I do appreciate the support you've shown for fine arts and am not surprised to hear that you had a good reason for what I mistakenly misinterpreted as disrespect. I feel much better knowing you meant no injury. Thank you very much for explaining, Matt

Because Matt knows Mrs. Kauffman, has experienced her support through his high school years, and knows her intention when it comes to him and his classmates, he responded maturely and graciously.

2. *Shared power*: Teachers and leaders must be willing to share power with students, parents, and community members. Power is like a candle. When you light someone else's candle, your candle continues to glow. As a parent or principal, we lose no power by sharing it with our children, students, or community members. Are there areas where students and staff can collaborate instead of a top-down approach? Sharing power with students can be as simple as letting students decide the design or logo of a club T-shirt. Students respond entirely differently when presented with a choice and a voice in decisions.

EYES ON CULTURE IN ACTION

Have students produce and deliver daily announcements: They have the best pulse on what is appealing to their peers and the most innovative ways to communicate important school news. Explain the parameters to them and let them know you are trusting them to handle the responsibility respectfully and earnestly, then turn them loose.

Encourage students to organize: Students can and should be encouraged to organize a club or group based on their interests, talents, or a social justice issue that is concerning to them. When students come to you with an idea, hear them out. Support the students by asking yourself and them: "What if?" and "Why not?"

Consult students: Do your students know your building goals? Do they know why they exist and how the goals impact them? Since it is their school, ask students about the building goals and student perceptions. Review school policies and procedures for input and different solutions. They have opinions and suggestions about course offerings and the texts used to deliver instruction. To achieve building goals, involve students, and get their ideas of how the staff can meet them. Focus groups that meet throughout the school year are an excellent way to elicit student feedback.

Negotiate with students on issues that matter to them: If your students want to participate in student-led protests, for example, talk to them about it. In recent times, many students have participated in protests centered around school shootings and racial violence. These are opportunities to listen, learn, and engage in a planned approach to enable students to raise their voices safely while also keeping the school on schedule and free of disruption. These are also opportunities to teach students what civil disobedience is and the consequences that come with that. Listen to students, their ideas, their fears, and problem-solve together. At a minimum, use the magic words, "Let me think about it."

Recruit students: Meet with and encourage influential students to promote the type of culture you want to see in your school. Staff identification of these influential students is one source, but make sure to ask members of the student body to identify those they consider influential. The staff and student-generated lists don't always match.

Share age-appropriate information: Let students know what is happening when a safety concern arises. Use plain language to share the information you have. If there is an ambulance in front of your school, tell students there is a student or staff member with a medical situation and that is why an ambulance is on campus. If the local authorities have asked you to lock your building down because of an event in the community (police chase, robbery nearby), tell your students what the police have asked you to do and why (this would apply to older students). Encourage students to text their parents and ask them to share information accurately. When school officials are transparent about issues impacting their schools, especially around safety matters, the level of anxiety and hysteria shrink.

Encourage participation in school and community events: Establishing a school-wide electronic bulletin board as a means to share opportunities with students is an efficient way to prevent a disparity of student knowledge when it comes to opportunities such as job postings, scholarships, leadership events, community and culture opportunities, and political participation.

Does Everyone Know The Standard?

Clarity of values is essential to promoting school pride. One pulse point that gives a clear indication as to whether the standards for student behavior and the culture you want everyone to enjoy has permeated throughout is the experience your guest/substitute teachers have in your classrooms. When guest teachers are sending students out of the classroom at a record pace and one referral after another starts to flow in, students are not meeting the standard. But do they know the standard? Have we been intentional in teaching those standards to everyone and have the students had an opportunity to practice them with teachers, coaches, directors, or administrators? Being clear about what we are going to do and what we are not going to do as a school is instrumental to instilling the shared values of our school culture.

A fellow PreK-5 administrator received this email from a guest teacher in his building:

Dear Mr. Duffy:

I will never again step foot in this building. The kids were rude, unruly, and disrespectful. They were disruptive and made it impossible to teach or for any student to possibly learn. Clearly, this is an ongoing problem since the teacher I was subbing for left me all sorts of notes about different students who she KNEW would be disruptive and disrespectful. Imagine my surprise when the teacher tells me AHEAD of time who would be a problem. You might want to get into that classroom more often. It's disgraceful.

What would you do with a note like this? Here are some things to consider as you face situations similar to this:

Teach the desired behaviors: Do you or your staff take the time to communicate with students what you expect of them when a guest teacher is present? Teaching students how to conduct themselves in your absence is likely more important than when you are present. Teach the procedures, assign helpers, discuss respect, explain the role of the guest teacher, and how important they are to the operation of your school.

Discuss the matter face-to-face with the classroom teacher: It is important to talk to staff members about the reports you receive from guest teachers. Notice we said talk—please do not email or text teachers about issues of this nature. The intent and tone in emails can be misconstrued. Ask some of these questions to get a clearer picture of the situation: What expectations have been shared with your students? How do you prepare your students for a guest teacher? How do you address the behavior issues of those students identified for and by the guest teacher? The teacher must know you are there to provide support, not criticism. It's a pretty sour lemon to chew on when teachers feel they are being blamed for student behavior. Developing a plan together to address student issues is a positive path forward.

Follow up with the students in question: Again, students innately want to be good and respectful but sometimes they do get sideways, especially if the standard for conduct is not clear or modeled. This is a good opportunity for leaders to reiterate expectations while also trying to learn more about what motivated the students to behave the way they did. Be careful not to overreact or underreact—just know that not responding at all reinforces the behavior that drove one of your guest teachers out of your building. None of us can afford to lose them.

Call the guest teacher: Acknowledging the note you received along with an apology goes a long way. It's a chance to communicate that the students were not meeting the standard and communicating that you followed up with the classroom teacher and the students. It will validate the feelings that prompted the note in the first place. Just know that the guest teacher will be out telling everyone in the community about their experience in your building. The phone call can change the negative narrative the guest teacher may be sharing about your school.

When students and staff know the standard, the experience for everyone involved is different and far more pleasant and productive. Read the letter below:

> *Hi Mr. Dillon,*
> *Just a quick note to let you know (again) what great students you have. I was teaching Spanish for a teacher who had 4th block prep, and I was asked to cover for another teacher in a different part of the building. As I'm standing there looking rather quizzically at a note saying room G217, one of your students asked if I needed help. I told her maybe so. She started to explain where the room was and then said, "How about if I just come back at the end of class and take you there?" She came back and we visited all the way to the classroom.*

1. *She's mature enough to read another's body language—I must have looked stumped.*
2. *She offered to go out of her way to help.*
3. *She made pleasant conversation while doing so.*
What a great young lady!
You're doing something right, Mr. Dillon!!!

The experience in this building was vastly different than the one in Mr. Duffy's, but understand, these same types of experiences can happen within the same building. That means there are pockets of excellence in which students and staff know and embrace the standard.

EYES ON CULTURE IN ACTION

Share the good news: Reach out to the helpful student and her parents (campus security cameras are a great resource to find the good things students are doing, not just their missteps). Thank the student for her kindness and helpfulness. Call her parents/guardians and share the positive report about their daughter's courtesy.

Reinforce the behavior: Include the guest teacher's message in your weekly staff memos as a great opportunity to share the benefits of reminding students about expectations when a staff member is absent and has a guest teacher. Share the same in your weekly student bulletin. **Note:** Especially at the secondary level, a weekly memo to students is a great mechanism to share necessary information (upcoming bell schedule changes, class meetings, registration materials, activities calendar). It is also a tool to remind students of their role in making the culture of the school one in which everyone can be proud. Sharing this particular message with the student body is a way to celebrate and reinforce the behaviors you wish to see from them.

Hire welcoming staff: It cannot be overstated how essential it is to have the most welcoming, helpful, patient, and kind people greeting others in every office, not just the main one. A middle school principal recently shared this situation:

One main office secretary was set to retire. I knew it was going to be difficult to replace her. She is everything you want when it comes to first impressions about our school. One of the applicants is a secretary in another building in our district. Through the interview process, it was clear that the internal district candidate had the most skills, but I wondered if she would do and say what she professed in the interview. I brought her back for a second interview to make sure she understood the expectations in terms of our school culture. I told her I had heard she can be negative and gossip about school matters. She did not react or become defensive. She didn't seem surprised. It confirmed that there was some truth to what I had heard, but I also believe in redemption. To be crystal clear, I said to her, "Here's what you need to know. I believe you are the most skilled candidate in the pool. I also know that all the skills in the world will not matter more than someone's attitude, kindness, and helpfulness. I want you to come here but you need to know that if you come here and are negative, gossipy, or treat people in a way that is contrary to my expectations, I will fire you." She responded, "That is why I want to come work here. I'm looking for a new beginning. I want a positive environment and I know I can do this because I want to be part of something special." I hired her and she has been a tremendous addition. She has taken her professional skills and contributed to the culture of our school because she truly puts students and staff as her top priority. She is an excellent example of how important it is for people to be in an environment that makes them feel valued and appreciated. She has been doing that for others since she joined our team."

Imagine the pitch to someone you are wanting to hire including the words, "I will fire you." The principal laid out the expectations, explained the standards and stated what would happen if the new secretary was unable to meet them. It also says a lot about the prospective secretary that she was willing to work for someone who made that hiring pitch. It says even more about the culture of that school that someone wanted to come there to be a part of something special.

We've Got Spirit, Yes We Do

The spirit and enthusiasm at the beginning of a school year are palpable. Students are happy to see their teachers and they are giddy about seeing each other. Hosting a pep rally on the first day of school is a game-changer. Skip the focus on rules, regulations, and procedures on that first day. Focus on school pride and teach your students what it means to "Carry the Banner." Pep assemblies can provide some teachable moments. Having older students teach the school cheers to the younger members is a great way to bring everyone into the fold of the school culture. Taking time to teach students what the National Anthem is, why it's important, and the etiquette that accompanies its playing helps students understand history and tradition. It minimizes disruptive student behavior during the National Anthem and is deeply appreciated by the community, most especially Veterans. Again, students want to do what is right; they want to be respectful. When the importance and meaning of the National Anthem are explained to them, they are more likely to bring that reverent spirit to the Anthem every time.

Consider this scenario:

> *A rival school sent their security team to a neighboring school to monitor their student section during the game. They are known for being a bit rowdy and slightly inappropriate in what they would chant or yell at their opponents. One student, in particular, treated*

his cheering that night like it was his job. He was loud, boisterous, and taunted players, officials, and our fans. The young man was repeatedly asked by their security staff to dial the negativity down. He couldn't manage to do that, so their security guard escorted him out of the building. As the security guard escorted the student out, the student kept saying, "What did I do wrong? We always do this!" A short time later about fifteen other student fans from their school packed up and started to leave the gym. Asked why they were leaving one student responded, "Because they won't let us cheer for our team." The security officer said, "We won't let you cheer, or we won't let you be negative?" The student responded, "Is there a difference?"

Yes, there is a difference, but they lost sight of that—in part because no one addressed what it means to be a fan and no one checked them when they were being negative and insulting to opposing teams, coaches, and fans.

Teaching students what it means to be a fan is worth the time and energy it takes to do so. Creating one voice from the student section is a tangible, positive experience for the athletes, marching band, drill teams, the rest of the fans, and the student section itself. But it isn't necessarily easy. Being a sports fan is personal and can be rooted in a deep passion for a sport, personal loyalty to the school, and student desires to support classmates. This personal investment can also result in a loss of perspective leading to poor fan behavior.

Poor sportsmanship on the part of the athlete, coach, or fan negatively impacts sports and takes a toll on contest officials, volunteers, security staff, and administrators. This has prompted schools to establish codes of conduct around sportsmanship. Additionally, in some cases, the spread of poor fan behavior is a result of an inconsistent set of rules for fan bases—both at home and away. Many school districts have adopted strategies to improve fan behavior. There is no better way to carry the banner for your district than proactively teaching everyone the standard of acceptable behavior at school-sponsored events. The public perception of your coaches, athletes, student bodies, administration, and the larger school community can be positive or negative and the steps taken proactively will determine those outcomes.

EYES ON CULTURE IN ACTION

Be welcoming: When guests from other schools arrive, how are they greeted? Does someone just hand them the key to the locker room and leave it at that? Or is there a student or staff ambassador to welcome the guests and escort them to the locker room?

Use banners and signage: Schools can reinforce desired fan behaviors while also communicating safety and security procedures through banners and signage upon entrance to school events.

Separate crowds: To the greatest extent possible, separate home and visitor fan bases to prevent altercations by using separate entrances and exits to reduce interactions between opposing fans.

Provide surveillance: Staff and security certainly need to be mindful of safety matters and alert to potential safety violations. Inappropriate and offensive behaviors need to be addressed and solid surveillance is an essential safeguard that can provide evidence if something goes wrong but also signals to fans that they are being monitored.

Promote respect for officials: The National Federation of High School Sports indicates 80% of officials quit (West, 2020) after the first two years on the job and unruly parents/fans are cited as the primary reason for stepping down. There is growing concern that the reduction in numbers of referees nation-wide will threaten the ability to offer varsity-level competition in some parts of the country. The number of licensed sports officials is down significantly in Iowa, for example. Total numbers of all sports officials peaked in 2010 at 5,274 but have fallen to 4,408 in 2019, an all-time low. (West, 2020). These statistics are playing out throughout the country. School leaders must deal with the unruly coach and fan behavior or run the risk of fewer opportunities for their students. Raising the level of awareness and concern for the critical state of securing officials should be addressed at both coaches' meetings and parent/guardian meetings ahead of each season.

Outline Acceptable & Unacceptable Behaviors: Use student groups to help their peers and parents understand what separates good fan behavior from bad:

Expected Fan Behaviors	Unacceptable Fan Behaviors
Be welcoming, hospitable to guests	Negative chants at guests, players, or fans
Be positive and maintain composure	Singling out or taunting opposing players or coaches by name or number
Respect officials and their decisions	Taunting/badgering officials for the calls made
Demonstrate respect for an injured athlete, no matter what	Profane, vulgar, or abusive language

Ask for help: Can your student body get too rowdy or offensive at a game? Talk to some of the student leaders and ask for their help. Encourage them to have fun but remind them of your school standards and ask if they would be willing to ask their peers to do the same. Students innately want to be positive, helpful, and perceived as good leaders. Do you meet with your senior class at the beginning of the school year? Leverage this by telling them that you are personally asking them for their help to set the tone and climate for the student body and the school year. They will rise to the occasion because they know you need them, they know you believe in them, and they want to carry the banner for the school in positive ways.

The Eggshell Culture and Retaliation

Positive and supportive relationships are the bedrock for the growth, development, and sense of safety for young people. How we speak to them, the conduct that we model or permit, and the values that we embody, are all critically important to the culture of a school and student programs. While this can certainly take place in the classroom, it need not be singularly focused on academic performance. Albert Einstein said, "The only source of knowledge is experience." It's important to remember that the most memorable student experiences often take place outside the classroom, but within the school setting. It is often through athletics, fine arts, service organizations, and clubs that students improve their ability to work with others, problem-solve, communicate effectively, and lead.

It should be noted that the **vast majority** of adults who work with youth do so with the utmost commitment to developing their students, athletes, or performers both personally and in their chosen activity. They care for their participants and do everything possible to provide opportunities for them that are rooted in care, compassion, growth, and equity. The youth feel safe in their presence, regardless of their personal performance. These adults teach when errors are made. They coach students up when they seem dejected. They listen and encourage. They give rides and provide equipment and food to those in need. They make sure their programs are inclusive and that all students in the program feel vital and valued. They are **all-in!** Unfortunately, there are times when the adults in the classroom, on the field or stage, or leaders of the school, use intimidation, fear, coercion, and ridicule to get students to conform to their expectations. In a small minority of adults, there is mean-spirited and abhorrent conduct toward students and even toward other adults. Left unchecked, this conduct does enormous damage to students and staff and the public's confidence in the school.

Take this scenario:

> *A volleyball player comes into a game to serve the ball and serves it right into the net. The coach raises his arms in frustration and pulls her immediately. On the very next play, another player shanks the pass and the coach immediately sends in a replacement for her. Does this approach help? What lesson did the players who were benched learn? They learned that they better not make a mistake or the coach would replace them at the drop of a hat (errr...ball).*

Not a single athlete, at any level, goes out to compete with a desire to perform any less than their personal best. When performers worry about making the slightest mistake or saying the wrong thing, the eggshell culture deepens. An eggshell culture is an environment that the participants are trapped by the fear of being ridiculed or called out by the coach. Coaches or directors who use fear and intimidation may scream at their team/cast members. They yank their performers at the slightest mistake. They are more likely to hurl insults than encouragement. They ridicule instead of teach. They are demeaning rather than demanding. Embarrassing their players/performers in front of others is of no consequence to them. They may even swear and engage in name-calling with language that can be racist, sexist, or homophobic.

When athletes are intimidated they fear potential consequences for not soldiering up to coaching expectations. This can range from the potential loss of playing time to an undesirable position change to removal from the squad. In the classroom, students can fear that a teacher will retaliate by judging their academic work more harshly or intentionally give a reduced grade. Detrimental adult behaviors in student programs can lead to negative and demoralizing experiences for students. Signs of detrimental adult actions include:

They need to be important and preferred: Adults who engage in bullying or retaliatory behavior are often insecure and unwilling to address their personal limitations so they take it out on more vulnerable people. They create alliances that make them the preferred adult to whom students turn and confide. They enlist other youth to engage in behaviors designed to demean or marginalize their target. They are willing to engage in inappropriate conversations to be perceived as "cool" and can encroach upon and/or cross appropriate boundaries of authority. They show little regard for their target's physical or mental health and can have a knack for making their target feel worse about themselves.

Private behavior is inconsistent with public persona: Retaliatory behavior often takes place in the adult's space of duty (classroom, field, court, stage) where students witness and experience it, but other adults often do not. These individuals can be friendly and disarming with other adults, including parents and principals, creating doubt that retaliatory behavior exists. Undermining the authority of parents or administration is not beneath them.

It is common knowledge but frequently denied: There is often a wall of silence about the adult's mistreatment of students, making it difficult for school officials to address the adult responsible for inflicting the bullying behavior. Students, colleagues, and even parents don't want to come forward because they fear retribution; however, students, teachers, and coaches often privately agree on which adults engage in intimidation and retaliatory behaviors.

When accused or confronted, the abuser distorts or minimizes their conduct: Under the guise of cultivating discipline, adult abusers often justify their behavior by insisting they are building character, tenacity, and work ethic. They will rationalize their misconduct, explain it away as a misunderstanding or a joke, and may even resort to lying about their behavior. And worse, they may blame the target for exaggerating or mishearing the insults or foul language hurled at them.

Other adults enable the abuser: Adult witnesses may deny any knowledge of reported inappropriate behaviors. In some cases, these adults are also intimidated and don't want to be involved for fear of retaliation by the abuser. They can convince themselves that they didn't see it, didn't hear it, and they feign shock by such accusations. These enablers often lie by omission.

Do you have students and families reporting to you that a staff member is demeaning, dismissive, intimidating, or abusive? When school leaders do not take such a complaint seriously, it can be traumatic and make people feel betrayed. Given that no teacher, coach, director, or administrator will readily admit to intimidation, retaliation, or creating an eggshell culture, this type of behavior can be difficult to prove. Students become accustomed to it, colleagues deny knowing anything about it, and parents are reluctant to come forward. Silence and secrecy become the perfect combination to embolden the abuser. It is for this reason that hiring people of character, whose honesty and integrity are without question, is essential to advancing a positive school and student program culture. When school officials, no matter their role or title in the organization, fail to treat all students with respect, dignity, and fairness, it must be confronted.

EYES ON CULTURE IN ACTION

Emphasis on personal development: On and off the playing field, in and out of the classroom, coaches and teachers are committed to the personal development of all students. Adults know the personal goals students have and design their feedback to help students reach those goals.

Student well-being is the top priority: Adults in the program are actively and transparently committed to the physical and mental health of their students. These adults create an environment that makes where they are the place students want to be.

Trust is evident: Students involved in the activity trust each other and their coaches/directors. The students are drawn to the adults and don't avoid them in an effort to stay off their radar.

Power is shared: Students have some autonomy and input regarding team norms and values. The students decide and can weigh in with their ideas and suggestions without fear of ridicule or retribution.

Adults hold each other accountable: Adults in the organization are committed to treating all students with respect and dignity and should someone fall short of the standard, another adult will intervene.

In Good Times...and Bad

Serving as a teacher or leader brings incredible moments of joy—they can be as grand as the kindergartner's first day of school, celebrating state championships, and witnessing students walk across the stage at graduation. The simple, everyday experiences with students also remind us how important the role of an educator is in the lives of children of all ages. Greeting students when they arrive each morning, talking with students in the hallway, participating in their pep rallies, and receiving heartfelt thank you notes are just a few examples of the simple pleasures of being an educator. For all the joy that comes with being an educator, there are some extraordinarily challenging and painful times, too. Across the country, school officials have had to deal with the devastation of tornadoes, hurricanes, and wildfires. Some have had the painful experience of leading students and staff in the midst of and after a school shooting. In 2020, every educator had to channel every ounce of inner strength to support students in the era of COVID. Neither teacher preparation nor educational leadership programs adequately prepare educators for such difficult or traumatic situations. One situation that we all will likely face at some point in our career is the death of a student or staff member. Navigating the empty desk in a classroom or the new teacher replacing a deceased staff member is delicate at best and agonizing at worst. From a high school principal:

> One morning I received a frantic phone call from the mother of two of my students. The older daughter, Mia, a senior at my school, was in critical condition after an early morning auto accident. Mia's younger sister, Mariah, had already reported to school unaware that her older sister had been injured. I took Mariah to the hospital and waited with the family as they prayed, against all hope, for their beautiful daughter/sister/granddaughter. Her injuries were devastating and she did not survive. It is incredibly humbling and extraordinarily painful to watch a family's worst nightmare play out before you. I couldn't possibly imagine the magnitude of pain Mia's mother, father, her two sisters, her brother, her best friend, or her grandmothers were experiencing. I could only imagine the level of support, care, and encouragement they would need in the months and years ahead. As this tragedy was unfolding at the hospital, I

found myself trying to anticipate the needs of students and staff as this reality became public.

As with all things we manage as school administrators, the death of a student or staff member requires our best efforts. It requires us to collaborate with others and to provide comprehensive support for families, students, and staff.

EYES ON CULTURE IN ACTION

Organize information: It is imperative to organize information and quickly assemble people to manage the crisis. The advancement of technology and social media requires us to quickly organize accurate information and distribute it appropriately and timely. School officials need to remain tight-lipped about virtually everything unless and until permission is secured from the affected family. Aside from the need to adhere to FERPA laws, in times of tragedy it is essential to follow the lead of the immediate family.

Rely on the crisis plan: We can't emphasize enough the importance of intimately knowing your crisis plan. Fortunately, the death of a student (or staff member) is not a frequent occasion—which means the crisis plan is not activated or utilized regularly either. School officials need to visit and revisit crisis plans to be prepared for such an event. There will not be a lot of time to respond, and if your plan is not crystal clear to the team, your response could be judged negatively at a time when your community needs your highest level of competence.

Establish point people: In this situation, it's important to establish point people to deal with media inquiries, the needs of students and staff members directly impacted, and the needs of the family as well. The media calls will start before names are even made public. Always remember: FERPA laws apply, even when tragedy strikes. Having solid relationships with local media, with other school communities, and with others who provide services to the school prove invaluable.

Identify most impacted: When a member of a school community dies, it is essential to identify those most closely associated with the student or staff member and to get to each one of them personally and inform them before the information is made public. School counseling teams need to immediately plan and announce the support available to the school community.

Respond respectfully: Counselors often assist in helping students organize a memory board, decorating a locker or classroom, or other tribute. It is essential to plan and discuss how to make the transition when it comes time to change the board and take down the notes and signs students created. Without clearly communicating the timeline and the plan for the student memorials, school officials set themselves up for being perceived as insensitive. Encourage counseling teams to let students know ahead of time that their writings/pictures/memories will be taken down on a specific date and will be delivered to the family of the deceased. Providing care and support for the staff is equally important. Meet together, share information that you can, provide grief counselors.

The death of a member of the school community is devastating. How we respond and reach out to those who grieve makes all the difference in the lives of those who, at that moment, need our very best. The school community can create moments of joy and peace even amid pain and sorrow. The extent to which school communities can serve others in good times and bad is dependent on one question all educators must ask themselves: "At this moment, am I touching the hearts of others the best way I can?"

Cultivating an Inclusive Community

Solving complex problems requires the ability to think in different ways and view identified problems from different lenses. There needs to be a diversity of experience and expertise when promoting an inclusive community—the administrator, teacher, counselor, parent, and the student each bring a different perspective. Educators must be willing and able to go to others to get perspectives different from their own to find a path forward for *all* students and staff. This is what those who carry the banner for their school do.

The premise of carrying the banner for our schools is that everyone is capable of, and responsible for, contributing positively to the school culture. While there is no greater need to experience the goodness of a school community than when tragedy strikes, it is the everyday opportunities to carry the banner that strengthens school pride and solidifies the community's identity. We carry the banner for our school by promoting a welcoming and inclusive community, where all members feel seen, heard, and valued.

Most communication is non-verbal and it is nearly impossible to determine the *exact* meaning behind body movements, facial expressions, quivering lips or eye maneuvers. It is, however, pretty easy to ascertain whether there is tension, joy, or apprehension between people based on non-verbal language. The next time you are at a large gathering, watch the reactions of people when other guests arrive. Making an intentional effort to observe the reaction of others will enable you to make observations about how people feel about those arriving. Some will suddenly become quiet or avoid interacting with those arriving. Others will move forward toward the person arriving with cheerfulness on their faces and outstretched welcoming arms. Even though a word hasn't been spoken, you can make observations about the relationships just by observing facial expressions.

These same types of observations can be made every day in schools, among the adults, between adults and students, and among students themselves. Do your students have friends at school to eat lunch with or turn to if they have homework questions? Do they respect the differences between them and generally treat each other with respect? Are staff members available to talk with students one-on-one? Do adults notice and acknowledge when students are doing positive things? Do the adults in your school treat students with respect? You can trust that students know when the answer is "Yes" to these questions and when the answer is "No."

To carry the banner for our students, we must truly assess their experiences in our schools. This requires schools to ask for student feedback and *really* listen. When students are invited to candidly respond about their experience at school, they embrace the opportunity and will do so with grace and respect. Sometimes with more grace and respect than the adults extend to them.

Take this scenario for example: A principal was distressed over the causal and pervasive use of the "N-word" among her students. The N-word was spoken between and among all races in the hallways and appeared in group chat messages for both class and student activity groups. The word was used in anger, "as a joke," and even as a greeting. The principal decided she needed to understand why this was happening and how it was making students feel. It resulted in several meetings with all students and some separate listening sessions for students of color. What started as a desire to understand how and why the N-word was being used among students launched into deeper conversations about race, and how students of color felt in that school. It resulted in the formation of a *Black Voices Matter* group, with a leadership council composed of students of all races. The group held listening sessions for students of all races and eventually surveyed Black students about the experience they were having at their school. There were three takeaways from the survey:

- Black students and their culture need to be more respected and appreciated.
- Discipline feels targeted at Black students.
- No Black teachers in the school; no courses on Black history, and teachers don't include a variety of Black culture or history in what they teach.

The student group worked collaboratively with school and community representatives to develop their mission statement:

> *To bring together a group of students at (insert school name) to empower and educate them about topics that matter to Black students and to get the voices of Black students heard in a respectful manner.*

They developed and practiced their "elevator speech"—the short synopsis they would give anyone to explain what Black Voices Matter is and why it exists:

> *Black Voices Matter is a new club that has been created to help make a change for Black students at this school who feel that they are not treated equitably.*

The group committed to including students of other races on the leadership team. Students had to apply, participate in an interview, and sign an agreement committing to their involvement. Applicants were asked to respond to the following questions:

+ Why do you want to be a member of the #BVM *Black Voices Matter* Leadership Council?
+ What do you feel makes a great leader?
+ How have you shown leadership? This could be a formal position of leadership (e.g. president of a club, small group leader at church, etc.) or an informal position of leadership (e.g. taking on leadership in a group project, persuading your friends not to participate in a risky activity, etc.).
+ Describe a time when you had to manage conflict. What was the situation and how did you respond?
+ What activities are you involved in? What are your interests outside of school?

Permitting the student group to proceed in the manner they deemed best was a culture builder in many ways:

> We cannot say we value the student's voice and then try to shut it down when their message is uncomfortable or considered controversial by some.

Gave power to their voice and their experiences: We cannot say we value the student's voice and then try to shut it down when their message is uncomfortable or considered controversial by some. The students in *Black Voices Matter* raised issues of concern for staff and administrative consideration. They bravely did so not because they desired to point out the problems of the school but because they have pride in their school and want a better experience for all students.

Opened the door for discussion regarding curriculum topics and texts used in classrooms: It expanded the discussion among staff regarding traditional texts used and how students of color experienced those in the classroom. It also opened the door for discussions around inclusive language more representative of all students and family structures.

Revealed that students of color felt discipline measures were more targeted at them: If the administrative team responded by denying their feelings or trying to counter their sentiment, the door would have been closed to further discussion and progress. Listening to understand yields greater results than listening to respond.

Provided a platform to talk through issues and surface their solutions: *Black Voices Matter* gave students a platform to share their stories and they effectively used storytelling in a unique way to teach, motivate, and challenge the thinking of others, especially the adults. The students identified their common challenges and collectively developed strategies to address those issues they viewed as problematic to their school experience.

When participating in a presidential town hall leading up to the 2020 election, Joe Biden was asked how he, a 78-year-old white man, could relate to and understand the concerns broadly shared among America's young people. Joe Biden responded to the young man who posed the thoughtful question by saying, "I view myself as a transitional president—a transition to your generation. You're the best educated. You're the most open. You're the least prejudiced generation in American history. The future is yours and I'm counting on you" (2020). In this statement, Biden was expressing boundless optimism and an eagerness to help usher along necessary change. As teachers and administrators, we have an opportunity to be transitional figures for our students.

Like Joe Biden, we are not of the same generation as our students, and therefore, may not be as comfortable or familiar with the preferred language used to discuss matters related to one's sexuality or gender identity, for example. That's OK—the important thing is that our students know that we are willing to listen and learn and evolve in our thinking.

We may not always get it right when addressing a student by his/her/their preferred pronoun, but that student will surely notice how we react once corrected. Are we defensive, dismissive, and avoidant? Or are we accepting, gracious, and intent on remembering for the future?

Students know when they are seen and valued by the adults in their building. Our LGBTQ+ students aren't asking us to be world-class experts on gender identity and sexual fluidity. They are, however, asking that their administrators and teachers see them, respect them, and carry the banner for them.

How we talk *to* young people *about* young people matters. Students are the reason for our work. They are this country's most precious natural resource and investing time, energy, and resources in them will pay dividends for our school communities and our greater society. They are going to make mistakes, have missteps, and simply behave in ways contrary to what is expected of them. Being a champion for all students means just that—*all of them*. Not just the ones who are easy-going, studious, or actively involved in school activities. Statements of inclusion delivered, posted, and modeled throughout a classroom or school create a community. Signage around a classroom or school serves as a tremendous reminder of what the community stands for and values. Here is one example of a welcoming statement which reveals what the school values and what is expected of all members of the community:

Welcome!

(Insert school name) aspires to create a welcoming and inclusive community that encourages, supports, and celebrates diverse voices

and perspectives. At this school, respect for differences is expected of all.

We honor the racial and ethnic diversity that enriches our community.

We respect the family structure, heritage, religion, and language of others.

We believe the culture, customs, beliefs, political affiliation, and economic status of others enhance our school community.

We value each person's sexual orientation and gender identity.

We support each other's special needs, learner differences, talents, and interests. (Insert school name) is your school. You are valued, and you belong here.

CHAPTER 5

Core Principle 4:
Be a Merchant Of Hope - Culturizing Empathy and Grace

As the story goes, there was an old man teaching his grandson about life. "A fight is going on inside me," he said to the boy. "It is a terrible fight and it is between two wolves. One is evil—he is anger, envy, sorrow, regret, greed, arrogance, self-pity, guilt, resentment, inferiority, lies, false pride, superiority, and ego." He continued," The other is good—he is joy, peace, love, hope, serenity, humility, kindness, benevolence, empathy, generosity, truth, compassion, and faith. The same fight is going on inside you—and inside every other person, too." The grandson thought about it for a minute and then asked his grandfather, "Which wolf will win?" The grandfather simply replied, "The one you feed." (Two Wolves, n.d.).

To be a merchant of hope in education is taking the small, simple moments or experiences that students, staff, or families have with your school and leave a lasting impression positively. It is having the capacity to help others bridge feelings of loss, inadequacy, or fear with opportunity, possibility, and relief. Being a merchant of hope is the ability to interrupt a pattern of self-doubt and instill confidence. It is supporting others to manage their emotions and find a path forward.

Currently, only a handful of states in this country have adopted comprehensive K-12 social and emotional learning standards, though more states are now adopting such standards to ensure that students learn important social-emotional-behavioral skills. There has long been a focus in early childhood to teach the "whole child" by supporting student growth in academic and non-academic arenas. By linking academic standards to social and emotional domains, state officials are broadcasting to teachers, parents, administrators, and students that these competencies are integral to students' future readiness for college, career, relationships, and responsibilities. Collaborative for Academic, Social, and Emotional Learning (CASEL) is a tremendous resource for those seeking to improve the social-emotional skills of both the students and the adults in the school community.

CASEL defines social-emotional learning (SEL) as "how children and adults learn to understand and manage emotions, set goals, show empathy for others, establish positive relationships, and make responsible decisions" (casel.org). Schools that lean into this effort are more likely to create caring, positive, and equitable learning environments that promote social, emotional, academic, and personal growth. At the heart of SEL work is empathy, the ability to recognize emotion in others and being able to understand the needs of others. Only when we understand the needs of others can we provide the support they need to be able to move forward. This is a critical skill and is essential to building trust. When we model empathy, trust increases, resulting in stronger and more positive relationships throughout the school. Oddly, empathy is rarely listed as a key leadership skill though recent research and evidence point to the impact empathetic leaders have on their organization's productivity and success. While empathy usually takes a back seat to other highly valued leadership skills such as organization, management, communication, vision, and goal setting, the absence of empathy will prevent the other skills combined to positively impact members of the organization.

Kindness, compassion, empathy, and love have recently been compromised by greed, suspicion, selfishness, and hate. This reality coupled with the increase in civil discord makes the work of teachers

> We need caring leaders now more than ever to do the right things the right way.

and leaders even more important. We need caring leaders now more than ever to do the right things the right way. Even though we cannot individually unravel the current societal conflicts, we each can certainly impact our school communities simply by the way we treat each other.

Empathy is greater than simply being able to relate to the feelings others have or the circumstances in which they may find themselves. It is more than kindness or pity. To truly exhibit empathy for others means we are willing to better understand what the feelings of another person are *and* understand what they need at that moment *without* judgment. Empathetic leaders can understand the personal or professional needs of their staff and are better equipped to provide the support and resources necessary to help the staff member move forward. Providing the personal and professional support necessary not only helps the individual, but also the entire organization.

EYES ON CULTURE IN ACTION

Know your staff: Empathetic leaders know their staff members personally—they know who their partners are and the names of their children. They know whose mother has pancreatic cancer, whose spouse was recently laid off, and whose sister just had a double mastectomy. They know these things because their staff trusts them and lets them into more than just their classroom. They let empathetic leaders into their lives. This results in leaders being able to better understand what factors are contributing to the effectiveness of others.

Embrace pain and discomfort: Empathetic leaders do not avoid dealing with the pain or suffering of others. They seek out those who are hurting by offering to listen, they text others to let them know they are thinking of them, they offer to remove burdens (let people come in late, leave early, swap schedules) so the one hurting can tend to their personal issue at hand.

Listen intently *and* open up: Being empathetic is the ability to be present to what's going on within that person *at that very moment* to understand their emotional state. Empathetic people listen to both verbal and non-verbal communications. Empathetic leaders understand that empathy is a two-way street and are willing to share their own emotions and experiences.

Help find a path forward: Even though leaders might not be able to improve a situation for a staff member, helping identify possible options to move forward and offering resources helps reframe the situation for them. Laying out options for consideration is appreciated when the one who is struggling is having a hard time thinking clearly.

Cultivate empathy in others: Empathetic leaders can develop collective empathy. They incorporate effective empathy education programs to help develop the emotional intelligence of children throughout their schooling years. They can help others go from, "I see you" to, "We see you."

If I Had Known

Reflect on the situation involving Jack, the student who announced he didn't prefer mom or dad being called because they were both deceased. What impact did that scenario have on you, your thoughts, feelings, and mindset? What was undoubtedly the most painful event in Jack's life may oddly become a moment of grace for us. It challenged us to observe more, listen deeply, and make no assumptions. It may help us determine how we can support and see others with an open heart and not make generalizations based on casual interactions or fleeting observations. Perhaps we can refine how we interact with students and how we approach them. We can no longer assume that the "traditional" model of families is the norm and we must create more awareness of the plethora of family structures and the need to validate each one. Although Jack's situation was extreme, it was a reminder about the responsibility each of us has to truly see our students and connect with them. If we strictly focus on student behaviors and consequences, we will miss opportunities to connect more deeply with students to be able to better meet their needs. We also miss opportunities for personal growth—personally and professionally. It validates that every child needs and deserves a champion. We may not be able to change student circumstances, but we can be that adult who embraces their stories. We can take those challenging and heart-wrenching experiences and do better for our students, families, and staff. We can bolster our commitment to withholding judgments about others, particularly around issues of behavior. If we must make assumptions about others, we can at least vow they will be the most charitable, benefit-of-the-doubt assumptions we can marshal. We can promise to make sure students, staff, and families feel heard, seen, and valued. We can give voice to the experiences of others and use the feedback provided as a venue to improve our school culture rather than defend our practices, regardless of their impact. We can be merchants of hope in the way we teach, lead, listen, apologize, and problem-solve.

The pandemic shined a light on how critical communication, collaboration, and trust are to the success of any relationship or organization. At the same time, the pandemic created incredible obstacles to connection, support, and motivation. COVID-19 also brought a lot of fear. The fear of people we care about getting sick—from loved ones to students to colleagues. Some of you reading this have already endured the worst of this through the loss of someone in your life. The death of a staff member or student hits a school community in powerful ways, COVID-19 or not. Educators throughout the country are exhausted and concerned about what the future holds. Despite the very best efforts of school personnel, some students have not been successful academically, some students have fallen through the cracks, and others have fallen off the radar. It is imperative to remember how important you are to your school, to your colleagues, and, most especially, to your students. They need you. They need your best (not your perfectionism, just your best). They need you to be their warm blanket—cozy, safe, and loved.

EYES ON CULTURE IN ACTION

Vote for yourself: Educators, by and large, spend their careers "voting" for others. They elect to call that parent, meet that student, change that lesson, or help that colleague. Yes, these are important and certainly contribute to the kind of culture that is discussed in *Culturize*, but it is perfectly fine for you to vote for yourself once in a while. Ask your colleagues and those who care about you for their support. Ask them (and accept) for feedback on what they think you could do differently that maintains your professionalism but also casts a vote for your well-being.

Stay on the beam: The education profession is a constant balance beam. The "to-do" lists grow, the feeling that you are working harder deepens, but accomplishing fewer tasks creeps in, and a physical toll can start to emerge—headaches, sleep disturbance, and more. The problem is, when these warning signs surface, we focus more on time-management when we should pay more attention to self-management. At some point, each of us falls off the beam and we only course correct out of necessity. We ignore the warning signs that our personal and professional life is out of order—the sleepless nights, racing heart, high blood pressure, anxiety, and depression. Most people attempt to get back on the beam only after they hit a wall, have a meltdown at school or home, or suffer a medical emergency of some sort. Set a time you are leaving at the end of the day and stick to it. Shut down email or cell phone at a certain time each night and treat that decision as though it were your job. And remember, most students don't go home and talk about the lesson you created or the task you gave them. They will report how they felt when they were with you. It's difficult to provide a good experience for others if you are not taking care of yourself.

Look for the joy: If you want others to benefit from your teaching or your program, find the joy in your work. Students know it, see it, and feel it when the adults at their school are tired, frustrated, and burned out. Every one of us has felt this way at some point but if you find that you look more forward to Fridays than you ever do Mondays, it's time to evaluate that. We *want* staff to look as forward to coming to school on Monday as they do going home on Friday, but we *need* staff to look more forward to Friday for their own well-being. If the personal life and well-being of a staff member are out of order, their effectiveness at school diminishes significantly. Yes, the accountability measures have increased and the resources have decreased. Everyone can get weighed down by that reality, but why are you an educator? What drew you to the profession? Have you maintained the passion, purpose, and pride in your work? Does your work bring you joy?

An Abundance Of Patience; A Minimum Of Pettiness

A friend used to conduct marriage preparation sessions for college students engaged to be married. She never felt she had the "expertise" to guarantee another couple would have a happy marriage but felt confident that these engaged couples could learn from other married couples at different stages of their married life. With each marriage preparation session, the marriage coordinator invited a panel of married couples, one married less than five years, one married 15-25 years, and one 30-40 years. Each of these couples would share their journey up to their stage in marriage. They would talk about finances, in-laws, holidays, and the different stages of parenting. They would share insights about how married life was unfolding for them to get the engaged couples to experience a bit of reality regarding marriage. During the friend's time as the marriage coordinator, she met a lovely couple who had been married for more than sixty years. Charlie and Dorothy were both in their 80's and as she got to know them better, she asked if they would be willing to speak to engaged couples. They leaped at the chance and participated in one of the panels. She relayed that it's incredibly heartwarming to be in the presence of a couple married for 62 years and to witness the joy, respect, and affection they still had for one another. The engaged couples asked them several questions and they gave several insightful, funny responses. To close out the session, Charlie and Dorothy were asked what they thought their recipe was for a strong, happy 62 years of marriage. Charlie didn't miss a beat, saying, "Our recipe is an abundance of patience mixed with a minimum of pettiness." Couldn't that be the recipe for every relationship in our personal and professional lives? As teachers and leaders, how can we take this recipe and create harmony and respect throughout our school communities?

EYES ON CULTURE IN ACTION

Expect manners: Adults in the school need to promote manners in the classroom, hallways, playground, and on the field or the stage. "Please" and "Thank you" will always override pettiness. Manners are a tool to cultivate empathy and positive self-esteem. Are there any children who relish feeling like the adults around them don't like them?

Promote respect: Monitor and address disrespectful tone and behavior (from students and staff) immediately. Be careful not to overreact with too much rigidity and strictness, but guard against underreacting by making excuses or justifying disrespectful behavior. Simply state, "We don't talk to each other like that in this class (school)." Not reacting at all is the worst thing teachers and leaders can do when someone is being disrespectful.

Be consistent: Are the teachers and leaders in agreement as to what disrespect sounds and looks like in your school? Do you use common language? Are teachers permitting disrespectful behavior while school leaders are not? Or vice versa? Students will divide and conquer if there is no alignment between teachers and leaders.

Address disrespect respectfully: When people are being disrespectful, we must respond with even greater respect. If a student is yelling and cursing, we need to get softer and more caring. Be careful not to ridicule, yell, or embarrass. Stepping aside with a student who is not managing himself well will be far more effective than calling them out in front of peers or other adults. These are teachable moments—address the behavior, re-visit your clear expectations, and discipline to the level of the infraction.

Set realistic expectations for behavior: Standards for behavior may differ child by child or adult by adult. If the expectation is higher than their capacity, it is not loving to expect them to be there without support and guidance. The student with severe ADHD may not respond well to a 60-minute silent reading session. The expectation for that student may need to look different. Forecasting potential disruptions and problems will support you in setting realistic expectations.

Know when to have conversations: When someone is being disrespectful, it's not the best time to have a conversation about expectations and consequences. Waiting for the dust to settle will yield better results.

Intervene early...and often: Children do want limits—it is a type of love language that says, "I care about you, I love you and I want you to have a future that is healthy, productive, and responsible." Having and enforcing rules is a pathway to developing self-awareness and self-management so they make positive decisions when we are not standing over them.

Correct and connect: Follow up is essential—when a student or adult behaves or speaks disrespectfully, the conversation afterward is critical. Students yelling at refs or calling out athletes from other schools? I can address that at the moment, directing students to stop. But it will be Monday morning when I meet with that student to explain my perspective, why I intervened, and what the expectation is moving forward. Pretend I have a body camera—what do you think we would see or hear if we reviewed this together? What thought patterns were you having at that moment that you could adjust or change?

Excellence In All Environments

People often use the words "excellence" and "perfection" interchangeably. In fact, excellence is from the Latin *excellere,* meaning "to surpass or excel." Expecting excellence from students or staff does not equate with expecting perfection. You don't have to be perfect to be effective. What a relief!

We get what we model. When adults look stressed, angry, or upset, students see and sense that. When conflicts arise between parents, the children know it even if the disagreement is not taking place in front of them. The same is true at school. Athletes know when coaches from different programs do not support or like each other. The drama students know when the drama director doesn't much care for the vocal music director or when one teacher has a negative tone with another teacher. When kids see adults at school dismiss or disrespect one another, they infer that such conduct is acceptable, despite the expectations that have been laid out for them. We lose credibility with students when we have one set of expectations for them but a different set among the adults. They feel the hypocrisy in what is said compared to what is done.

Of even greater harm is when teachers and coaches marginalize the students they're instructing; screaming at athletes for making mistakes, for example, or shaming kids in the classroom, underscores a message that there is one set of rules for the adults and a different one for students. When this is what is modeled, you can be sure the students will armor themselves in whatever way possible—defensiveness, dismissiveness, negativity, or guardedness—to avoid being the subject of this adult behavior. At this time in their lives, when the world is often harsh, your classroom, court, stage, pool, or field should be their refuge. How can we be someone students call or come see when they have news to share or someplace to go when the world is harsh? Can we be excellent with our students when we are not willing to also be that with our colleagues?

We make a lot of judgments about situations, people, or experiences. Many of us make hundreds of decisions in a day—decisions about curriculum, instruction, behavior, culture, lesson/play/practice plans, and much more. As adults, we must be careful about the judgments we make regarding students and each other. It's always intriguing when students and parents inform school administrators that the incoming class is "the worst class" ever. Sometimes the "worst" label says more about the adults than the students. Teachers and school leaders must guard against judging someone's excellence by their entrance or their exit. We must take time to nurture and encourage those who come to us lacking confidence or courage or with a history for which they may not be proud. Each year we host a "Students 1st" banquet at our school. The purpose of the event is to recognize and celebrate students who have overcome some sort of obstacle or challenge to successfully finish high school by improving their attendance, academic performance, or behavior. It is one of the most moving experiences for both the students and their families (who are invited to attend). Additionally, the student honorees identify and invite a staff member whom they reveal as someone who influenced and supported them. Here is what one recipient wrote about what the honor meant to her:

> *The actions that I have made in my past do not define who I am now, for I am stronger and will walk into my future knowing that the young 14-year-old girl who walked these halls will be a woman who walks out of college with a new look on life knowing her past actions are not her defining ones.*

Someone who felt eternally judged by adults could never write something like this. Regardless of the "scouting report" we receive about another adult, student, or group of students, let's withhold judgment until we get to experience who they are for ourselves. That is the best way to ensure that we give our best to them.

Giving our best cannot be limited to our work environments. If all your excellence goes to everyone at school, there will be nothing left to give at home. A word to those with a strong work ethic (aka workaholic): You know who you are—the first to arrive and the last to leave school, those who send emails all hours of the night, and those who simply cannot stop thinking about work. We know who you are, too. We have stood in your shoes. We have loved our work with students and staff as much as the next person, but we do not have to choose between giving our best in one environment versus another. We can give it to both so long as we are intentional and make considered decisions. We want to caution you and share with you that you cannot give excellence in the work environment without also giving it at home. When our families get our time and energy, our school family also benefits. When we set aside time to be present for our families, our school family will know that they should be doing that as well. Close the computer, put the phone away, stop grading, drawing up plays, or reviewing rehearsal notes. Put it all away for whatever designated time you set and just be with your family or friends. As leaders, we have a responsibility to help those relatively new to the profession to recognize that their responsibilities at home are as important (or more important) as those at school. For staff members in committed relationships, remind them they are first a partner. If they're a parent, remind them they are second a parent. To hear directly from the "boss" that those two roles must take priority over their role as teacher, coach, or aspiring administrator sends a very clear message about what matters most. That one conversation says volumes about the culture of their workplace and its impact cannot be understated.

EYES ON CULTURE IN ACTION

Prioritize and re-prioritize your time: You and your colleagues may not have the same perspective on work-life balance. In *Culturize*, life-fit is described in detail regarding how educators reduce their work-related stress while balancing personal circumstances free of guilt or judgment. Life-fit recognizes that this concept looks very different for the staff member with a newborn at home, the coach with a sick parent, or the director whose spouse suffers from mental illness. Find ways to support your staff members during their times of tribulations—a note, phone call, just stopping in their office or classroom to ask them how they are doing.

Set boundaries: Our line of work is serious but it ought not to be so serious that it consumes our waking moments at the expense of some leisure or family time. Educators get pushed and pulled in unimaginable ways, but it is the inability or unwillingness to set boundaries that results in burnout, fatigue, illness, bitterness, and resentment. Who wants to come home to that? Set boundaries with your email, phone calls, texts, and drop-in visitors, and remember the only people who get upset about your boundaries are those who benefit from you having none.

Find time every day to unplug: Author Anne Lamott famously said, "Almost everything will work again if you unplug it for a few minutes, including you." (Lamott, 2017) Support and encourage colleagues to do the same.

In the movie, *The Bucket List*, auto mechanic Carter Chambers (Morgan Freeman) and billionaire Edward Cole (Jack Nicholson) develop an unlikely bond through the time they share in the same hospital room. Against doctor and family advice, the two set out to complete things they always wanted to do. At one point in the movie, Morgan Freeman said, "I believe you measure life by the way others measure their life with yours." What does that mean to you? In what ways do you think others would want to measure their life with yours? In what ways would others avoid measuring their life with yours?

A Word On Courage

The opportunities to live courageously exist every day, but anxiety, stress, and discomfort often get in the way. Personal courage doesn't have to mirror Rosa Parks' level of courage or the courage of firefighters who stormed into the burning twin towers on 9/11, but for some, everyday courage can feel just as daunting. It takes courage to acknowledge what you want out of a long-term relationship or to explore different job opportunities, but doing so requires informing the partner or the boss of your plans. Some people struggle to have candid conversations and spend more energy avoiding them than what would be required to just have the discussion. People are often scared or intimidated to speak their truth so they choose the "comfort" of the stale relationship or the unsatisfying job. These are the "avoiders." A friend recently joked that her daughter was such an avoider that she worried she would end up marrying her boyfriend just so she didn't have to break up with him. While that is an amusing example, it underscores how uncomfortable and scared people are with taking the courageous steps necessary to live their truth. The world is full of opportunities to speak up and step out of situations that require courage. Examples include:

+ Challenging racially or sexually offensive comments.
+ Initiating a prayer with a partner or your family.
+ Letting someone go—either in a personal relationship or in the workplace.
+ Interrupting negative talk about students among colleagues.

While we may not be able to fix everything, courage requires us to take steps to do something to course correct. What difficult conversations have you been ducking out of fear for the other person's reaction? What message have you withheld for fear of the reaction or retribution? What action have you not taken because it makes you feel uncomfortable? Developing courage takes time, it takes practice, and it takes experience. Mostly, it takes a willingness to confront the fears you have about potential outcomes.

EYES ON CULTURE IN ACTION

Accept responsibility: There is no way any of us are getting out of this world without having to partake in some act of courage. Being an educator requires us to be courageous in our words and deeds and when we avoid this responsibility, we let the entire organization down.

Listen to internal sirens: What inappropriate or ineffective practice have you witnessed or has been reported to you? When we see or hear something that does not align with the values of our school culture, there is an internal siren telling us that the issue must be addressed. Understand that "issues" can quickly become incidents or controversies. Either way, you will end up having to deal with it at some point and it's far more manageable when it is just an issue. When something does not sound right or feel right, it probably isn't and needs to be addressed.

Practice with others: As mentioned before, talking things over with other people helps formulate thoughts and frame the courageous discussions to be held. Because there is inherent angst when having to address an employee about performance concerns or explaining to a parent why their child didn't make the team, practicing those conversations with others organizes thoughts and provides confidence. Giving feedback to others is a skill that most people don't automatically have; it is something we must practice.

Model for others: Take others under your wings. When you need to speak with a staff member about complaints received from parents, include associate/assistant principals in those conversations so they can learn.

Do The Kindest Things In The Kindest Way

On any day of the year the denominator of kindness will be vastly greater than the numerator of cruelty.
Daniel Goleman (2016)

Perhaps some of the incivility in our culture right now is a result of a cultural shift away from benevolence, the impulse to do kind or charitable acts for others. When we engage in acts of kindness, we change the way we view ourselves, others, and the world. Kindness increases self-esteem, lowers blood pressure and cortisol, a stress hormone which directly impacts stress levels (Siegle, 2020). Not surprisingly, kind people experience more gratitude, joy, peace, and hope. Simply put, when we engage in acts of kindness, we feel better.

While "random acts of kindness" and "pay it forward" have become popular and promote generosity, they can also result in transforming how we treat one another. Organizations have been formed just to promote kindness. Researchers have studied the effects of kindness on individual health and books upon books have been written about why and how kindness matters. There is even a *World Kindness Day* (November 13) sponsored by the World Kindness Movement. Why so much emphasis on kindness? Because it truly makes a difference in the heart, mind, and spirit both for those extending the kindness *and* those receiving it.

Kindness is about extending empathy, embracing differences, and promoting tolerance. Kindness means we first look for the good in others rather than pointing out their failures. Being kind is a form of self-discipline and is not always easy, especially when dealing with rude people or others who have mistreated you. Being rude is easy. People cut you off when driving, barge in line ahead of you at the store, or worse. But there will always be greater decency and goodness, even when indecency and viciousness exist.

Honesty, responsibility, and respect are cornerstones of effective leadership and healthy relationships, but in the end, nothing matters more than kindness. It is the kindness and care provided by adults that nurture students and makes school a place they *want* to be. How we treat each other determines the type of community we offer to students, staff, and families. It determines how students and colleagues feel about teaching and learning at our schools. There are opportunities for simple acts of kindness every day in our schools.

When good people work collectively, goodness and kindness become the norm. The spirit in which you give determines how you receive. If you give joyously and generously, you will receive abundantly.

Students at every age are living in a social media era that can be pretty harsh. Keyboard warriors ridicule their coaches, teachers, and administrators with false and personally attacking comments. They mock those who think, look, and vote differently than they do. Eleanor Roosevelt had wise words for this phenomenon long before it even existed: "Great minds discuss ideas. Average minds discuss events. Small minds discuss people." If children are to grow up valuing kindness, it must be modeled by adults. They need to witness kindness that is sincere, generous, simple—and frequent.

Educators across the country are working harder than ever. They want to do right by their students and provide the very best educational opportunities. They use their knowledge to open the hearts and minds of their students. It doesn't matter how hard we work, how right we are, how smart we are, or how much power we have, kindness trounces everything. Kindness doesn't require making monumental changes to every classroom, school, or student activity, but it does require each of us to make some small gesture or speak words to make a difference to just one person at a time. We can use praise and polish to remind our students and staff of their value. Some students will require just a little more polish every now and then to eventually shine.

There are no *Eyes on Culture in Action* recommendations to close this out. Just be a good person. Help where you can, give what you can, and always do the kindest things in the kindest way. To serve as a merchant of hope requires kindness above all.

CHAPTER 6

Handling with Care

I f you have ever had to pack up a house for a personal or family move, you know how daunting and overwhelming the task can be. If you are fortunate enough to be able to hire movers, the task becomes more manageable. Making sure special and fragile items are clearly marked with a "Fragile" or "Handle with Care" sticker is essential to successfully move precious items from one location to another and alerts the movers that the contents inside the boxes are fragile and likely special to the owners. When movers are hired, there is an expectation that the handlers will be cautious and protective of the contents being moved. Handlers will respond to the "Handle with Care" alerts in their unique way. Some will proceed with caution, taking special care, while others will strictly focus on accomplishing the task, regardless of how jostled the items may get in the process. The difference between the two handlers rests in their approach. The cautious handler is mindful that the items belong to someone else and wants them successfully moved, fully intact. The other is focused on task completion without regard for the outcome.

In the context of this book, we encourage you to assume that everyone in the school community has an invisible "Handle with Care" sticker, reminding us that, at times, everyone can be fragile. To avoid being a thoughtless or insensitive handler, we need to recognize that how people feel, observe, and respond can vary. There are many examples throughout this book that are designed to challenge educators to embrace the opportunities presented every day to support and challenge students, staff, and families in respectful and dignified ways. We live in a world that suggests using power and authority to handle others is the preferred way. Focusing on personal care, empathy, respect, and dignity can be challenging in this societal context, but it is absolutely essential in our schools.

The four core principles of *Culturize*—Champion for Students, Expect Excellence, Carry the Banner, and Be a Merchant of Hope—invite educators to find ways to make a positive impact to leave a lasting impression on students, staff, and the larger school community. As school leaders, our words, decisions, and how we care for others determine the quality of our schools. Educators who concentrate on and commit to the four principles of *Culturize* nurture a vibrant school culture rooted in genuine and caring experiences for all members of the school community. Given the amount of time our students and staff spend in classrooms and on our courts, fields, stages, and playgrounds, don't we want all students, teachers, coaches, and directors to walk away grateful for the experience and sad that it has come to an end? Unfortunately, far too often students and staff are more thankful that it's over. They are ready to move on and often never look back, at least not favorably. None of us wants our own children, grandchildren, nieces, or nephews to have that experience and it takes all of us, collectively, to provide opportunities for other people's children that make them grateful they are part of our schools. Much like first responders, we need to be alert, accessible, and attentive to those who need to be handled with care.

In our own lives, there may be times when we need to be "handled with care" because of personal difficulties and challenges. Imagine, if during times of difficulty or pain, we attached to ourselves a label marked "Handle with Care." It would alert everyone we encounter that they should proceed with sensitivity when interacting with us. One is left to wonder the level of care Jack would have received if he had a "Handle with Care" sticker. The trajectory of his school experience changed as his school years progressed, but no one knew of the tragedy of his life.

If we knew when and who needed to be handled with care, we would be better able to provide adequate support. However, do we need that visible evidence when someone else is hurting to champion for them? Do we need a special notification to prompt us to expect excellence from ourselves and others? We can carry the banner for our schools when we assume the best about others and invest in relationships with students, staff, and colleagues, ever mindful that each of us is called to serve. As merchants of hope, we must continue to believe in every student and every adult, every day, and be willing to do whatever it takes to inspire them to be more and do more than they ever thought possible. As you move forward in your journey, remain committed to extending grace and empathy to meet the needs of all members of the school community by handling them with care today, tomorrow, and always.

References

Alber, R. (2016, June 29). *Getting Curious (Not Furious) With Students*. Edutopia. https://www.edutopia.org/blog/getting-curious-not-furious-students-rebecca-alber.

Aspy, D. N., & Roebuck, F. N. (1983). *Kids don't learn from people they don't like*. Human Resource Development Press.

Braun, H. (2019, October 31). *The 4 Faces of Misbehavior and What They're Trying to Tell You*. The Classroom Key. https://www.theclassroomkey.com/2015/12/4-faces-misbehavior-theyre-trying-tell.html.

Brice, L. (2013, August). *Lee Brice - Don't Believe Everything You Think - YouTube*. YouTube. https://m.youtube.com/watch?v=5cr4oYF7QAE.

Brown, B. (2017). *Rising Strong*. Random House USA.

Casas, J. (2017). *Culturize: every student, every day, whatever it takes*. Dave Burgess Consulting, Incorporated.

Daniel Goleman on the Negativity of Daily News. SuperSoul.tv. (2016, July 20). http://www.supersoul.tv/supersoul-sunday/daniel-goleman-on-the-negativity-of-daily-news?TW=tw_omag_daniel_goleman_negative_news.

Dreikurs, R., & Grey, L. (1993). *Logical consequences; a handbook of discipline*. Plume Books.

Gladwell, M. (2020). *Talking to strangers: what we should know about the people we don't know*. Penguin Books.

Goleman, D. (2020). *Emotional intelligence*. Bloomsbury.

Graaf, J. D., Wann, D., & Naylor, T. H. (2014). *Affluenza: how overconsumption is killing us - and how we can fight back*. Berrett-Koehler.

Joe Biden NBC Town Hall Transcript October 5. Rev. (2020, October 6). https://www.rev.com/blog/transcripts/joe-biden-nbc-town-hall-transcript-october-5.

Knost, L. R. "*When little people are overwhelmed by big emotions, it's our job to share our calm, not to join their chaos.*" - *L.R...: Parenting quotes, Quotes, Kids and parenting*. Pinterest. https://www.pinterest.ch/pin/437552920048626863/.

Maynard, N., & Weinstein, B. (2020). *Hacking school discipline: 9 ways to create a culture of empathy & responsibility using restorative justice*. Times 10 Publications.

Medina, J., Benner, K., & Taylor, K. (2019, March 12). *Actresses, Business Leaders and Other Wealthy Parents Charged in U.S. College Entry Fraud*. The New York Times. https://www.nytimes.com/2019/03/12/us/college-admissions-cheating-scandal.html.

Pierson, R. (2013, May). *Every kid needs a champion*. TED. https://www.ted.com/talks/rita_pierson_every_kid_needs_a_champion?language=en.

Quotes, A. L. (2017, April 1). "*Almost everything will work again if you unplug it for a few minutes, including you.*" ~@ANNELAMOTT. Twitter. https://twitter.com/AnneLamottQuote/status/848286102331031552.

Reeves, R. V. (2018). *Dream hoarders: how the American upper middle class is leaving everyone else in the dust, why that is a problem, and what to do about it*. Brookings Institution Press.

Rittenberg, A. (2020, June 12). *Iowa's Kirk Ferentz admits 'blind spot' on black players' issues, vows to improve environment*. ESPN. https://www.espn.com/college-football/story/_/id/29304234/iowa-kirk-ferentz-admits-blind-spot-black-players-issues-vows-improve-environment.

Ruiz, M., & Wilton, N. (2012). *The four agreements: a practical guide to personal freedom*. Amber-Allen.

Schmoker. M (2004). *Learning Communities at a Crossroads: A Response to Joyce and Cook* **Phi Delta Kappan.** 86(1), 84-89.

SEL is... CASEL. https://casel.org/what-is-sel/.

Siegle, S. (2020, May 29). *The art of kindness*. Mayo Clinic Health System. https://www.mayoclinichealthsystem.org/hometown-health/speaking-of-health/the-art-of-kindness.

Sinek, S. (2011). *Start with why*. Penguin Books.

Two wolves. (n.d.). Retrieved February 18, 2021, from https://www.firstpeople.us/FP-Html-Legends/TwoWolves-Cherokee.html

West, B. (2020, April 21). *Plight of Officials: Inside the ref decline*. TelegraphHerald.com. https://www.telegraphherald.com/sports/local_sports/article_0fc10156-f806-5637-a17c-de7daef52ecf.html.

About the Authors

Jimmy Casas served twenty-two years as a school leader, including fourteen years as Principal at Bettendorf High School. Under his leadership, Bettendorf was named one of the Best High Schools in the country three times by Newsweek and US News & World Report.

Jimmy was named the 2012 Iowa Secondary Principal of the Year and was selected as runner-up NASSP 2013 National Secondary Principal of the Year. In 2014, Jimmy was invited to the White House to speak on the Future Ready Schools pledge. Jimmy is also the author of six books: *What Connected Educators Do Differently, Start. Right. Now. – Teach and Lead for Excellence*, the best-selling book *Culturize – Every Student. Every Day. Whatever it Takes, Stop. Right. Now. – The 39 Stops to Making Schools Better, Live Your Excellence: Bring Your Best Self to School Every Day* and his latest release, *Daily Inspiration for Educators – Positive Thoughts for Every Day of the Year.*

Jimmy is the owner and CEO of J Casas & Associates, where he serves as a professional leadership coach for school leaders across the country. In 2019, Jimmy launched ConnectEDDBooks, with his partner Jeff Zoul, a publishing company aimed at giving back to the profession by supporting educators to become published authors.

Joy Kelly has more than twenty-five years of educational experience in public and parochial schools as a teacher, coach, mentor, associate principal, and principal. In 2015, Joy was named the Iowa Associate Principal of the Year. She also provides coaching and training for new administrators in Iowa. Joy serves as a leadership coach for administrators across the country on behalf of J Casas & Associates. Joy earned a Bachelor's degree in History from The University of Iowa, a Master's degree in Educational Leadership from The University of Northern Iowa, and is a licensed PK-12 superintendent; she also has an Educational Specialist (Ed.S.) degree from The University of Iowa.

Joy has presented on topics related to school culture at state and national conferences, including NASSP and ASCD. Joy believes the culture within a school is dependent on strong connections among all members of the community, rooted in kindness, respect, and dignity. Joy maintains that the culture of an organization is directly related to its performance and that the responsibility for cultivating meaningful relationships throughout the school rests with all members of the community. Contact Joy via Twitter at: @joykelly05 or email: joymkelly5@gmail.com

More from ConnectEDD Publishing

Since 2015, ConnectEDD has worked to transform education by empowering educators to become better-equipped to teach, learn, and lead. What started as a small company designed to provide professional learning events for educators has grown to include a variety of services to help teachers and administrators address essential challenges. ConnectEDD offers instructional and leadership coaching, professional development workshops focusing on a variety of educational topics, a roster of nationally recognized educator associates who possess hands-on knowledge and experience, educational conferences custom-designed to meet the specific needs of schools, districts, and state/national organizations, and ongoing, personalized support, both virtually and onsite. In 2020, ConnectEDD expanded to include publishing services designed to provide busy educators with books and resources consisting of practical information on a wide variety of teaching, learning, and leadership topics. Please visit us online at *connecteddpublishing.com* or contact us at: *info@connecteddpublishing.com*

Recent Publications:

Live Your Excellence: Action Guide by Jimmy Casas
Culturize: Action Guide by Jimmy Casas

Daily Inspiration for Educators: Positive Thoughts for Every Day of the Year by Jimmy Casas

Eyes on Culture: Multiply Excellence in Your School by Emily Paschall

Pause. Breathe. Flourish.: Living Your Best Life as an Educator by William D. Parker

L.E.A.R.N.E.R. - Finding the True, Good, and Beautiful in Education by Marita Diffenbaugh

Educator Reflection Tips Volume II: Refining Our Practice by Jami Fowler-White

Disruptive Thinking in Our Classrooms: Preparing Learners for Their Future by Eric Sheninger

Made in the USA
Middletown, DE
17 May 2021